Jacek Tylicki
Art and Artworks

Introduction by

Leszek Brogowski

Jacek Tylicki - Art and Artworks

www.tylicki.com

ISBN-13: 978-0985369231
ISBN-10: 098536923X

Published by: 21UNIVERSE

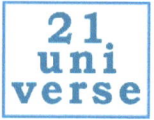

SPONSORED BY

Front cover art:
"Give if you can - Take if you have to"
Stone sculpture/installation. Arambol, India 2009

CONTENTS

Leszek Brogowski

DISINTERESTEDNESS OF ART — ANONYMITY OF MEANING

Anonymous Artist and other artistic actions
of Jacek Tylicki

"Instead of pursuing, in Art or by means of Art,
a world which is not yet visible in our every day
reality, hedonist aesthetics seeks instant
gratification (...)"

R.Rochlitz, *Esthètiques hédonistes*,
                    "Critique" # 540, May 1992, p. 354

I.

If a given artist's art projects a path, a coherent unity that could be called a world-view (*Weltanschauung*), if it can first reveal, and then defend on its own terms, a certain vision of the world, then grasping this vision, which is understood as a holistic project, is the most fundamental way of shaping our attitudes toward the meaning of all the pieces, works, and projects which effectively contribute to shaping this path. Thinkers and poets of the Romantic era, especially Novalis and the two Schlegels discovered that apart from aesthetics, which focuses primarily on the effects of the mental satisfaction derived from Beauty, there is also the possibility of creating an art criticism (which in case of these thinkers meant predominantly literary criticism), which turns to the work of art itself for categories and criteria necessary to the analysis, or the evaluation of the work. Therefore, a natural flow of interpretation must progress from the experience of the first gaze — the one which seizes the wholeness but is still clearly intuitive— to the aesthetic categories that would enable us to uncover all the specific meanings coded inside each particular project. Only in the end could we compare and find correlations between the meanings which were found by means of this procedure, and our original intuitive sense of the whole artistic path. The senses and the meanings constituted and determined in this twofold way should reinforce one another; if any tensions remain they must be considered as an invitation to further interpretative work.

It is with this methodological awareness, progressing, gradually, by small steps, that we will try to approach the senses and the meanings of Jacek Tylicki's actions and realizations. A clue guiding us in this endeavor will be a certain quality characteristic to most —if not all — of Tylicki's projects. Let us call it for now "disinterestedness", though it is obvious that in the course of our inquiry we'll have to further explain how this term can be applied to art. For instance Tylicki's living in a tree was disinterested in some sense, as was his free distribution of intriguing pieces of art produced by New York artists to the public. Also disinterested, in yet another sense, was his building a giant handless clock on Mount Esja in Island, as, finally, was his attempt to make the work of a contemporary artist anonymous.

A certain degree of disinterestedness can be found even in a venture launched by Tylicki in 1986, which consisted of a business, i.e. a money-making activity conceived as an artistic action. At first glance the idea may seem provocative, if not blatantly iconoclastic. However, it is in a humanistic spirit that Jacek describes his project, the meaning of which is worth a deeper scrutiny in the context of the most fundamental questions about ways that today's artist needs to explore in order to function in modern societies. What are the contemporary models of an artist's work and existence; what mechanisms relate economic and political systems to the material and ideological aspects of art? These are problems which must not be underestimated in the light of the present crisis of western culture in general, and more particularly the crisis of the art market, the universal fiasco of the art gallery, the threatened position of government subvention systems, and other conservative reactions to art: we are in the early days of making crucial decisions about the future existence of art.

This is what Tylicki said about his project: "I wanted to show that an artist can be more universal in choosing his activities, that he is not circumscribed by narrow specialization and the frequently rather banal posture of "starving artiste", a creative individual who's totally at the mercy of the art market. I simply wanted to make a point that an artist, like any other person, has an enormous, sometimes hidden potential for being more than a mere "object" subjected to the all-labeling system of modern education, the work market, and the very strict boundaries of specialized disciplines. I strongly believe that a great surgeon can be at the same time a marvelous musician, or perhaps also a decent pilot.[i]

But why would a surgeon want to be a musician? Why would anybody want to be an artist?

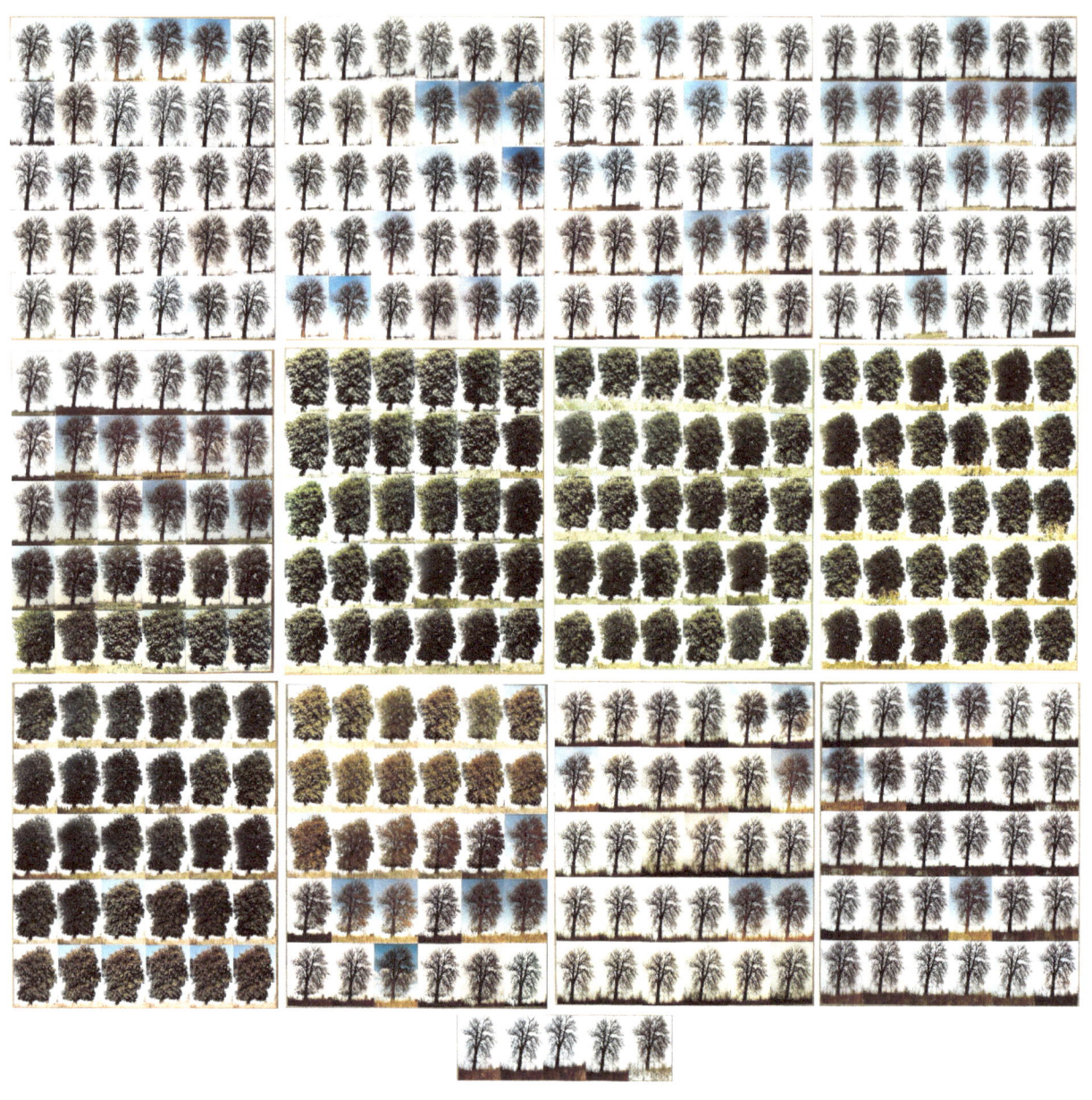

365 days of a tree
1979. Lund, Sweden.

II.

First of all let us ask ourselves if art doesn't define itself through a certain disinterestedness and if this disinterestedness isn't in fact a very specific quality of art? Right away we are confronted with a paradox. If indeed art were a disinterested activity it would mean that we make it for no specific reason; furthermore, that while making art we distance ourselves from all *possible* motivations. We make art — if art is an expression of disinterestedness — not for financial gain, not for pleasure, not to learn anything, and not out of a need to express or disseminate any message. We will see a little later that the same situation can be interpreted from another point of view: we can say that an artist is motivated by an internal necessity, or that art is an expression of a certain freedom that can be experienced in art and through art-making. If art is disinterested then the reason we cultivate it is that it is art. That is all. Art is art for its own sake, it is art for art.

The above conclusion, formulated so early in this process is at the same time very radical. Therefore it has to be taken with some reservations. For instance, we mustn't try to connect it with the conceptualist definition of art, such as the following formulation of Joseph Kosuth: "the only purpose of art is art itself, art is the definition of art[ii]. The similarities between two statements can indeed be misleading; however, despite appearances their meanings are very different. Our thought was brought into focus by questioning motivations: why are we engaging in art-making, what are the values that attract us to art and what is the rationale behind it? Finally, more specifically, what is the message that can be derived from Jacek Tylicki's art?

If the idea of art-for-art's sake is the answer to this question then we cannot escape the paradox: we make art "for no use" or no good reason. However, let us entertain for a minute another idea and ask ourselves what if we abandoned art altogether, forgot about making art? What's the difference? If when we're creating art we are doing so for no reason, certainly for no one's sake, no gain, not even to achieve some very noble purpose, and toward no concrete result.

In 1979 Jacek Tylicki decided to live in a tree. This provided an experience which became a very informative illustration of his faith in a certain value of disinterestedness. At that time it was perhaps still more of an intuition than a program formulated with a full awareness; something we can deduce from Tylicki's self-commentary made during this period. "I lived in a tree for a few days" — he wrote. "What was my motivation? Visual poetry? Or was it only a response to the increasingly logical Universe that is incessantly gathering speed? I'm sure it wasn't merely a wish to escape; it was a suggestion.[iii] A careful reading of this commentary unveils both the need and the impossibility of justifying such an enterprise: the action was indeed disinterested. Disinterestedness is here a motivation and, at the same time, a complete lack of motivation. We know of cases when someone decided to live up a tree for a concrete purpose. For example "Glen Woodrich spent 182 days up in a tree in *Golf and Amusement Park* in Norwalk, California, from January the 1st through July the 2nd 1978.[iv] Both gentlemen lived in their trees, independently and so far as we know without any knowledge of one another's ventures. However, the difference between living-in-a-tree-as-art-project and living in a tree with the goal of making it into the "Guinness Book of Records" resides precisely in this very specific disinterestedness, the meaning of which we are now trying to capture. Glen Woodrich's living in a tree represents an exploit with a clear purpose of scoring the record with consequent annotation in the book of world records. In this case a relationship to Nature serves only as a pretext for an extreme achievement and the record. Jacek Tylicki's living in a tree is a reaction to the twisted relation humans have with nature, a response to a predominantly one-sided and single-streamed development of the World as well as to the destiny of mankind in this World.

Without doubt, the concept of disinterestedness, as it relates to the emergence of the idea of art for art's sake in the late eighteenth century, had its origins in the profound loss of traditional functions and grounding that art and artists previously received in bourgeois society.[v] Certainly the social dimensions that made art focus primarily on itself, the isolation, or perhaps even the alienation of art from the social aspect of the cultural tissue, feed the compulsion to hang onto this narrow and quite limited conception of art. We can view the tautological definition of art given by the conceptualist artists (quoted above) as the culminating point of this tendency. It is however interesting to observe that for many artists, bringing their art to this ultimate brink resulted in their stepping to the other side; as a consequence they found themselves moving from "purely" artistic positions to positions which could best be described as "purely" political.

To make art or not to make art — to be or not to be an artist — cannot mean the same, because we make art not to satisfy our vanity but for art's sake and no *other* reason. As in a real true love where the reckoning of all possible motivations is always

disproportionate to the intensity of our feelings. Perhaps more poignantly than it resembles nihilism, aesthetic disinterestedness resembles a certain theological situation such as an attempt to define the absolute, i.e. god. Indeed, man tends to depict the absolute as a perfect and autonomous being, independent of any external factors, and most importantly, as the source of all existence. According to the German philosophers "*Das Grund ist ohne Grund*", while the French maintain that "*la raison est sans raison*" thus making an equivalence between the absolute and the rational. We should also remember the scripture: "I am who I am". In all its premises art similarly rejects every "why" or "what for". Art is that which is. Could it be then that art is its own only and self-sufficient reason? The paradox of disinterestedness resolves itself in the absolute: in this configuration art would represent the absolute of human culture, the absolute which could not be justified by any reason outside art. This really lays the foundation of modernist aesthetics, which in response to the withdrawal of religion from the cultural landscape, will grant art the status of New Religion and gradually transform it into a space of lay Sacrum. According to Walter Benjamin art, sensing the approaching crisis "reacted with the doctrine of *l'art pour l'art*, that is, with a theology of art. This gave rise to what might be called a negative theology in the form of the idea of "pure" art, which not only denied any social function of art but also any categorizing by subject matter. (In poetry, Mallarmé was the first to take this position.)[vi] We must therefore consider the full complexity of the following configuration of concepts: disinterestedness — the tautology — the artistic absolute; in that light the complexity of Tylicki's attitude toward conceptual art also becomes clearer. On the one hand it would be difficult to reduce his projects to a limiting tendency, one which defines art within narrow boundaries of semiotics, while on the other hand Tylicki takes various discoveries of conceptual art for granted (especially the possibility of formulating art with different "languages" and "materials") treating them as a natural horizon of contemporary art creation. A similar remark applies to the Sacrum of art: for Tylicki art is a domain of disinterestedness but it is not the absolute. It is much closer to a quintessential creative human activity.

Benjamin's point of view seems to be one-sided in a twofold way. Firstly for historical reasons: it clearly demands that art should be justified by well-defined social functions. The experience of Social Realism showed the dangers hidden behind such a stipulation. Secondly, because from the very beginning we can raise an objection to the arguments of Benjamin's reasoning: what if the alienation of art is only a result of social and cultural reshaping which doesn't leave space for certain core values, or for certain types of reality that in fact constitute live elements of art? It is not art which abandons social service, but society that slowly rids itself of art. Or perhaps art became alienated precisely because the world turned hostile to its value, and its isolation was falsely interpreted as a pretension to be called a new religion or an earthly absolute.

If this is true, we should now try to elucidate the meaning of disinterestedness as an aesthetic category without falling into the usual trap of creating artificial distinctions such as: professional occupations versus hobbies, or disinterested music-making versus interested (i.e. fee-based) medical care.

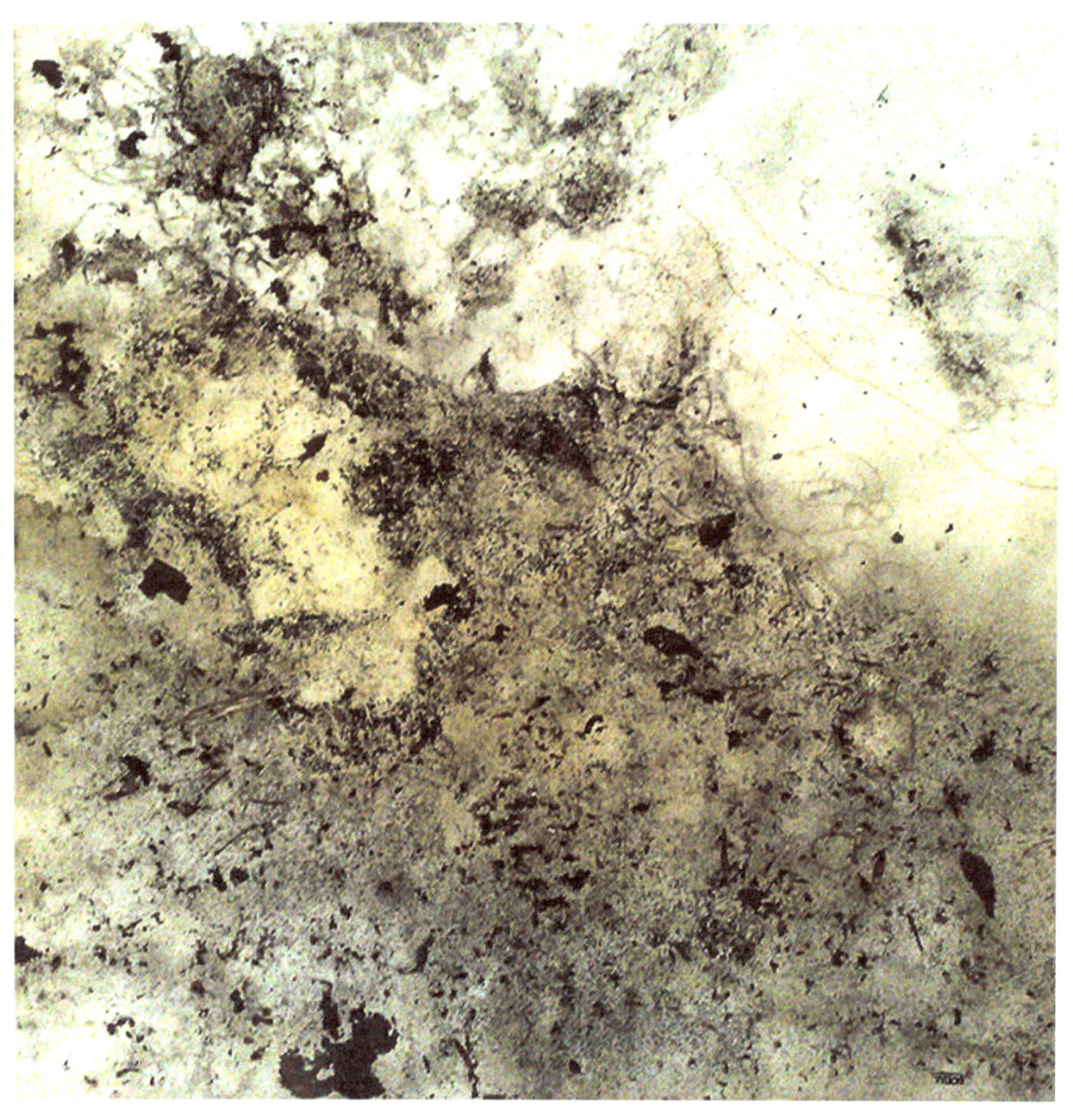

Nature No. 1

4 days in the grass of the meadow.
S.W. of Lund. Sweden. June 16 – 20, 1973
460 X 460 mm. Watercolor paper.

III.

Since disinterestedness seems to be, at least on first glance, a common characteristic of several of Tylicki's actions, as well as a general quality of numerous art projects, we are led to bring into play a certain archaeology of *disinterestedness*. However, rather than looking for the origins of disinterestedness, understood as an aesthetic category, in the Christian concept of Grace, we will turn our attention to Kant's "Critique of Jugement". The idea of disinterested delight appears in the first of four definitions of beauty and the aesthetic disposition of man is defined in these terms: "Taste is the faculty of judging of an object or a method of representing it by an *entirely disinterested* satisfaction or dissatisfaction. The object of such satisfaction is called *beautiful*.[vii], wrote Kant in 1790.

So how can delight be fully dis-interested and at the same time remain a pleasure and, therefore, have a certain "interest"? We immediately stumble against the same paradox in many contemporary art projects whose authors frequently emphasize the disinterestedness of their actions while adding that their work seeks to renew the social fabric, to enliven the mind, etc. Aren't these "interests"? A reflection upon this question may enable us to uncover a humanistic stake in the occupation of art formulated by Kant and thus shed light on the intuitions lying at the core of both the attitude promoted by Jacek Tylicki and the vision of the world which is projected by the way he lives his art.

Kant consciously introduces the paradox of a disinterested interest; paradoxes have always served as a springboard for thought. However his philosophy gives a very precise definition to the aesthetic meaning of disinterestedness. I am facing a beautiful object (for Kant this could be equally a contemporary or an old art object, a natural object, a landscape or even — though he never formulates it himself — a beautiful girl or a boy). If an object causes my delight as *beautiful* then my attitude must be disinterested in two ways. First of all it has to be the source of a purely aesthetic satisfaction, that is, it must be free of desire. A beautiful object does not delight me because I want to possess it. But there's also another meaning of disinterestedness. Though a beautiful painting seduces us by the sense of the spectacle it spreads before our eyes in a concrete, sensual shape, the meaning here represents more than a mere play of concepts. Aesthetic delight must be also disinterested in intellectual terms: beauty, according to Kant, is an experience which can neither be fully rationalized nor contained within sterile concepts. There is always something incomprehensible, inexplicable about beauty. Kant adds that "*Beauty* is the form of the *purposivenes* of an object *without any representation of a purpose*.[viii], which is yet another way of referring to aesthetic disinterestedness. The latter could be understood in the following way: confronted with a work of art we feel the artist's intention to convey some kind of meaning;

however any attempt to read it would almost necessarily fall into an infinite spiral of self-renewing interpretations. The viewer has to accept that a need to understand connected with the experience of beauty can never be satisfied. Also the cognitive aspect of this experience must remain disinterested.

In fact for a viewer who follows the rule of aesthetic experience there are no other solutions. Again, according to Kant, the essence of such experience consists in specific awakening of all the complex work of our faculties; a beautiful form enlivens them by uniting principles of reason and impressions of sense. When Jacek writes that his living up a tree was a response to "the increasingly logical" world he points to a familiar feeling, which many of us share. It is the feeling that human existence in modern civilization has become barren and that the elaborate system of sheaths, wrappers, and screens separates us from our cosmic roots. In 1964 Herbert Marcuse presented a similar analysis of being a one-dimensional man in the frame of a highly developed industrial society. In aesthetic judgment, which according to Kant resides within the imagination, the senses and reason abdicate, giving away their independence. "And by an aesthetical Idea I understand that a representation of the Imagination which occasions much thought, without, however, any definite thought, i.e., any *concept*, being capable of being adequate to it; it consequently cannot be completely compassed and made intelligible by language.[ix] In its aesthetic function imagination is both the perception of the senses and of reasoning, but it is not either of them if considered separately. An aesthetic idea — a form of art — could indeed be conceived as a result of the perfect synthesis of "a man of senses" and "a man of reason" into one, un-fragmented human existence which is inviolable in its integral totality. Imagination is the site as well as *the source* of this synthesis while art is the product and the native land of the synthesis.

So how can we ultimately define aesthetic disinterestedness? Obviously, it must not be simply identified with acts of grace even though a choice made in the name of some "higher" values is necessarily involved in disinterested actions, especially if by higher values one can understand allowing oneself to experience a new dimension of the specific wholeness and integrality of *one's own* existence. It is therefore an interested disinterestedness whose interest is focused on the multi-facetted fullness of human existence.

Little by little, we can begin to understand a previously cited statement of Jacek Tylicki in which the author talks about every artist's "potential of being something more" than a mere actualization of *possibilities* dictated by modern society. By virtue of this declaration art can be understood as a path that could lead the modern *man or woman* to find and experience the forgotten fullness of being, and the lost harmony of self-experiencing. According to Jacek, who alludes to a utopian model of art, everyone should be an artist in order to experience a transformation. Everyone can be an artist but only very few actualize that potential.

Two questions directly ensue from our considerations. Firstly, if art had transformative power over human life then the experience of fullness would have to be *communicable*. But in what way can the artist put us, the viewers, on the right track toward this unique experience, the experience which enables him to discover his own multidimensional fullness of being? Secondly, if in the light of the above reflections Jacek Tylicki's artistic activities begin to take shape as a coherent, holistic stance toward the world, we still need to show how to create the possibility of *the passage* from what was previously said here about imagination and beauty to the contemporary condition of art, which underwent fundamental changes during two centuries that have passed since Kant formulated his Critique of Aesthetic Judgment.

We will now address these issues.

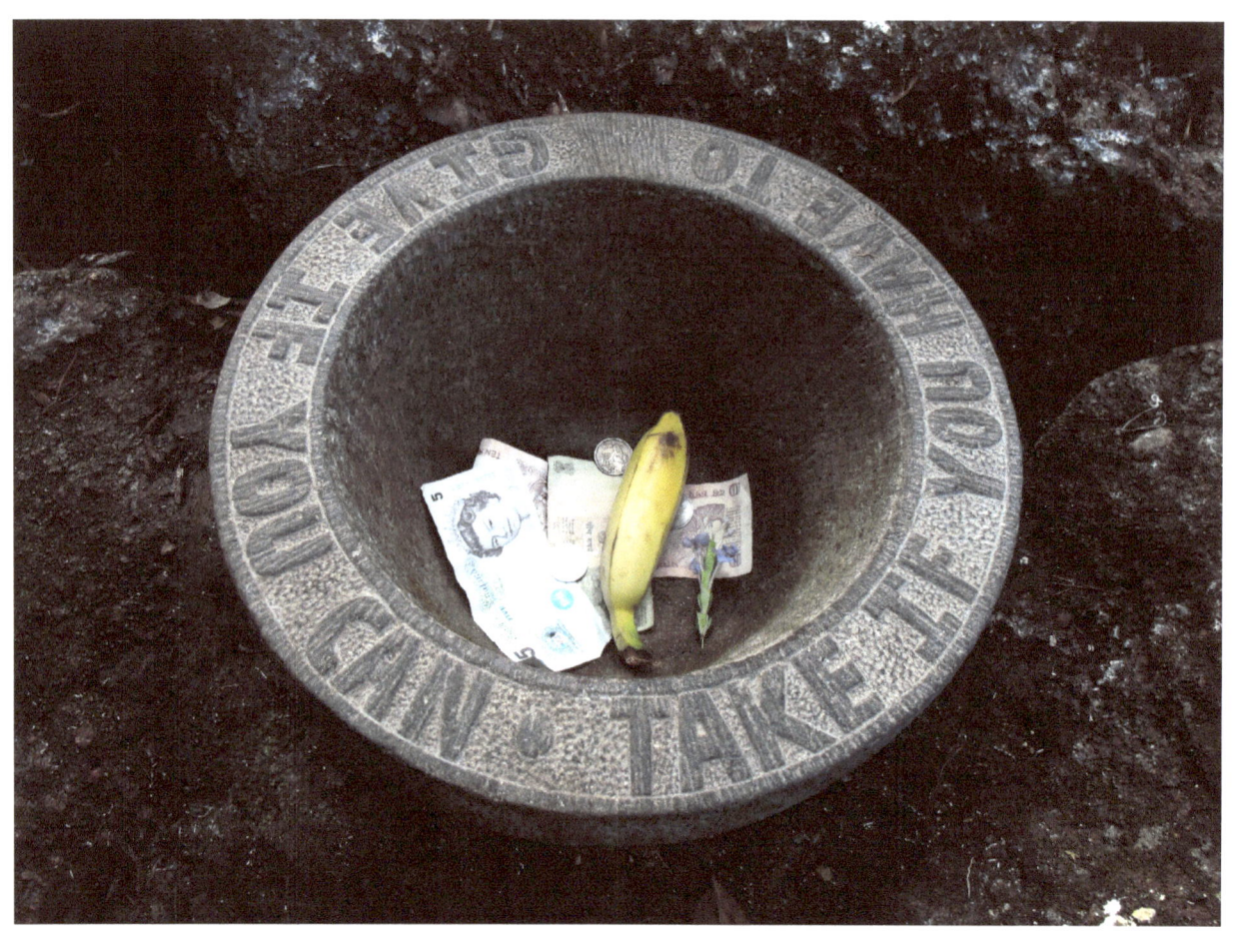

"Give if you can - Take if you have to"

Stone sculpture/installation.
Arambol jungle, India 2009

IV.

This is why the humanism outlined by Tylicki's art allows us to think of the human community not only on the grounds of the universality of beauty, but also because through art we now open a new prospect of meeting with nature. In this manner art can be included in the aesthetic experience of universal communicability and, at the same time, get reconnected with the aesthetic experience of nature. We must not fall into the trap of restricting modern humanism to the classic Renaissance definition of humanity *by emphasizing its opposition* to the natural state; on the contrary, the new humanism has to achieve a renewed alliance with nature. The universal ethics of modern humanism emerges from a horizon shared by all the beings inhabiting the Earth: the necessity of preserving nature.[x] The above-mentioned project, as well as many other Tylicki's works in nature are his own contribution towards rethinking humanism in art, on a scale that is broadened to match our contemporary times. We must come back to this thought in our further considerations.

In the meantime however we must address a growing doubt as to whether or not our implicit generalization of Kant's ideas about beauty can be successfully adapted to our views on art in general, and more specifically to the contemporary experience of art.

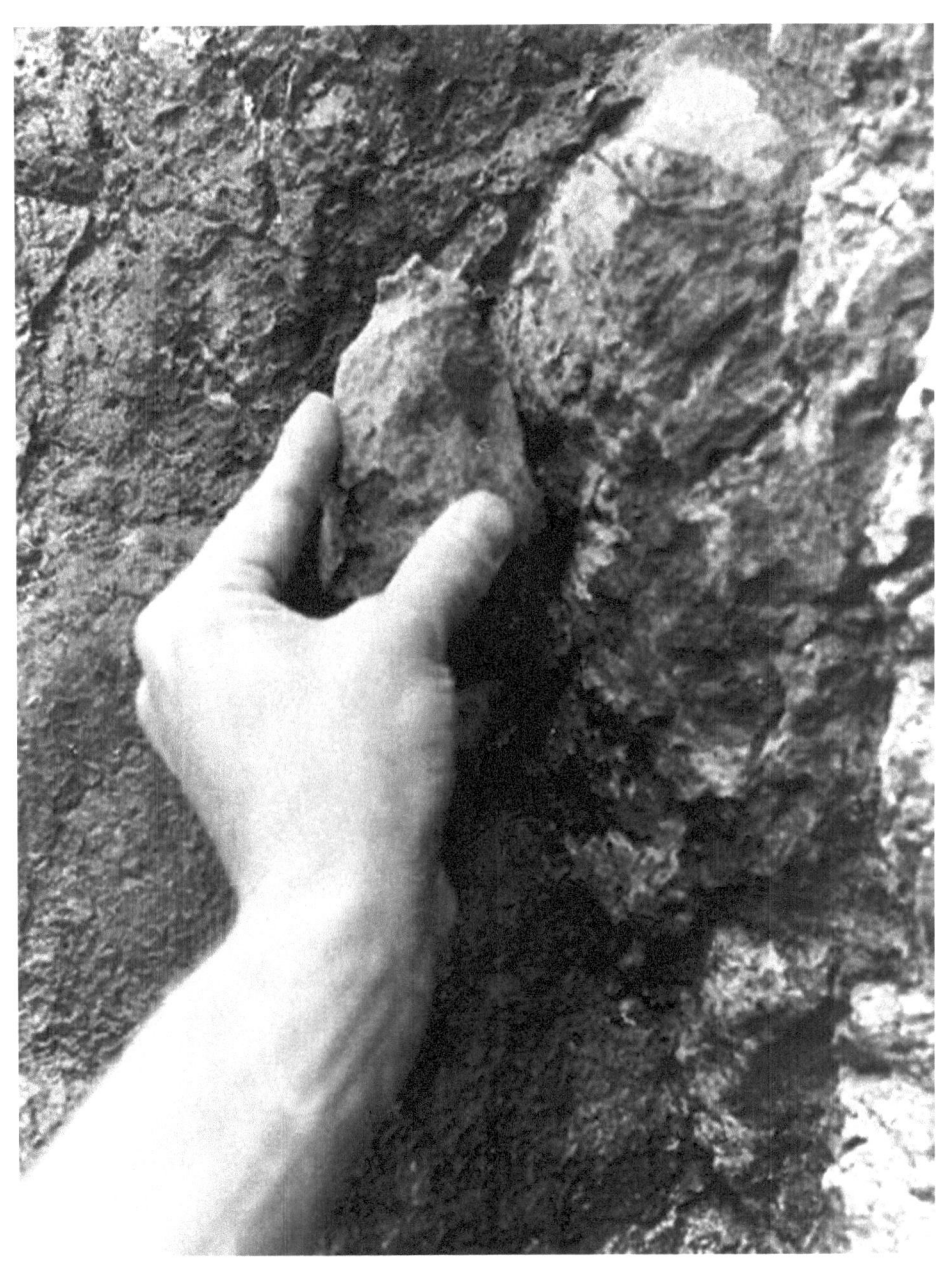

*Reconstruction attempt of the
Korpfulfssadir Quarry* (Iceland 1979)

"It took seconds to dynamite the hole in the otherwise virgin Icelandic landscape. For many hours I tried to fit back one single stone - with no results".

V.

So can we still apply these reflections on beauty to contemporary experiences of art? And if so, in what ways? One of the most likely candidates for a link between the philosophy of Kant and modern art seems to be the concept of game.[xi] As we saw earlier in this article, Kant himself used the term of a playing (which is conceptually similar to "a game") while talking about "a free play" of intellect and imagination. Schiller took one more step in the same direction: a play as such constitutes the experience of plenitude and harmony with the world reserved only to childhood, by means of which art enables man "to combine the greatest fullness of existence with the utmost self-dependence and freedom.[xii] Developing Kantian thought, Schiller distinguishes two main inclinations of man: a drive for change, which is a need to constantly seek satisfaction from sensual and emotional content, and a drive for the preservation of one's form, which is a need to be oneself, to be a person, to allow one's own existence to sustain a certain identity. Schiller also discovers a third inclination, which is the drive to play. Because of its central positioning as a middle term put in between two other drives, the drive to play is subject to the influence of the others in such a way that the needs of the senses nullify the need for rational exigencies, while the exigencies of reason negate the contingency of the sensations. Therefore, in playing, man achieves a double freedom; liberated from both the contingency and the necessity, he is at the same time morally and physically free. "For (...) Man plays only when he is in the full sense of the word a man," — wrote Schiller — "and *he is only wholly Man when he is playing.*[xiii]

Schiller broadens the problematic by pointing out that if art has the humanistic value assigned to it by Kant, it is because the idea of play lies at the core of art, and it is in art that playing wholly realizes its purest form. Beauty therefore is included in the experience of playing, but the essence of the aesthetic experience is provided by play, not beauty.

The concept of playing gains immense significance in aesthetics and later reaches far beyond its territory. However in his book, conceived as a manifesto: "Homo ludens. A Study of the Play Element in Culture" (1938), Johan Huizinga notices that "since the 18th century art, precisely because recognized as a cultural factor, has to all appearances lost rather than gained in playfulness.[xiv] Huizinga rightly exposes a very interesting fact: as the concept of play enters art theory, art itself progressively loses its ludic quality. Looking in the opposite direction, Jacek Tylicki seeks to capture anew the aura of spontaneity, while in the theory of art we begin to observe a split between two distinct meanings of the word *das Spiel*; aesthetics clearly distances itself from the meaning of play as a complete engagement of humanity, and introduces the idea of playing conceived as "the mode of being of the work of art itself" (Gadamer).[xv] The later thinking of conceptual art will develop in this spirit. At the beginning of this essay we consciously introduced an opposition of two ideas: conceptual tautology and disinterestedness. It seems that conceptualism aspired to be simply the semiotics of art. Conceptual art paid for opening itself to new forms of art by repressing existential experience — traditionally thought of as the source of artistic creation — and reducing art exclusively to an inter-subjective space of meanings. Today, still, Kossuth declares: "To have a work of art we do not need a physical object, but in order to realize this, we have to make a clear distinction between the play of art and other forms of playing. (...) A work of art is essentially a play within the meaning system of art.[xvi] Play in this context is merely a possibility in a semiotic field and not a maximal realization of human possibilities.

Originality and the present day interest of Jacek Tylicki's art can be found in his synthesis of artistic humanism, which has its origins in the need for the most authentic experience of a complete human existence, which has been expressed by art since Romanticism, and the contemporary critical reflection of art upon itself and its own cultural conditioning. In his work art projects a way to unite elements perceived today as contradictory, but which in fact are considered as such only as a result of the fragmentation of some original, yet long forgotten or nearly effaced, fullness and unity of human existence. Such contradictions, artificially imposed, can be found in abundance in our culture. In this brief exposé of Jacek's art we've already brought up several examples of opposing concepts, ideas, which the artist tries to overcome through his work, such as for instance: the opposition between senses and reason (*Living in the Tree*), thoughts and feelings ("*For a chicken, the most beautiful is chicken*[xvii]"), artist and non-artist (*Business as Art*), art and nature (*Natural Art*), or art referring to one's own existence and socially oriented art. While using modern art forms, such as action (happening), intervention in Nature, photographic documentation, installation, operation on economic mechanisms, etc., Tylicki remains interested in a certain authenticity, which involves existence, experience, and political views.

To be accurate, the Kantian concept of imagination conceived as a mysterious power, which reunites thoughts and sensations, corresponds to a figure of the old alchemical process, where inside Paracelsus' alembic all oppositions resolve into a perfect unity. The idea of the unity of contradictions influences the entire tradition of German Idealism and the poetry of Romanticism. In Jean Paul's poetry night represents the alchemical alembic; love plays a similar role for Novalis. In art the function of a symbolic alchemical vessel is fulfilled by imagination for Kant, or play for Schiller. A great follower of the romantic tradition, Joseph Beuys, considered art to be continuous work toward the reconstruction of the unity of existence — the forgotten fullness, whose loss is now recognized as the origin of the present crisis of our civilization. The artist consciously occupies a place at the center of this crisis and becomes a living symbol of reconciliation between the unities broken by the culture: soul and body, the mystical and the political, reason and folly, nature and culture, art and life, etc. Beuys believed that division is both a tool and a prerequisite of successfully implemented power. This is why the church and the state are always interested in fragmenting human beings, in dividing body from soul, artist from non-artist. However, the essence of art lies in the opposite: the completeness of human existence. Such fullness can be seen by the official powers as a threat because of its superabundant strength, which in consequence exposes art as deeply political.

And it is Tylicki's intention to create art which would constitute a political fact in the original, Greek sense of the word, where political means indeed a thing of many (citizens): *poli-teia*. From this perspective the actions of Tylicki, disrupting a socially accepted order of things — such as for example the scheme of material dependency between the artist and the art gallery (*Business as Art*), the concept of monetary parity of the works of art (*Free Art*), the custom of placing a capital value on the artist's name (*Anonymous Artist*), etc. — are clearly political facts in the most fundamental sense. Skirting round the extremes, these facts represent neither a political program, nor a narrowing of politics to so-called professionalism, but constitute facts relevant to all of us; facts which concern the true meaning of art, its values, and its place in our society. They can be called political because by challenging the status quo they invite reflection and initiate changes of outlook.

However, the moments, where contradictions are reconciled, very palpable in Tylicki's work, have other sources. His long sojourns in India, where Tylicki stayed on three separate occasions, gave him an opportunity to encounter the philosophy of the East, in which the unity of infinitely internal and infinitely external, Brahman and Atman, the complementary nature of Yin and Yang, represents the fundamental principles of all being.

In a way, Beuys' program can be read as a response to the criticism of disinterestedness of art formulated by Walter Benjamin. It has certain utopian characteristics — after all, Utopia is only another form of art's commitment to humanism. "A map that does not include Utopia is not worth even glancing at", said Oscar Wilde. However, art is not utopian in the sense that its experience of human power is only an illusion. Art resembles Utopia because the program of transforming the human

mind which it postulates is a never-ending task. But if it were to be completed, in any form or shape, art would lose its *raison d'être*: "(...) probably art would become useless, or rather we should all be artists[xviii], wrote Bergson in 1900. Also Breton could not agree with the Marxists, believing that the first thing that has to be changed is mind; the world comes in the second. While this of course seemed like a Utopia to the Marxists, the recent turn of the historical process means that we are back to the stage of transforming (or this time maybe repairing) the mind, where our dramatic attempts to defend nature from complete destruction gives Utopia a new meaning.

The art of Jacek Tylicki is not meant to be a program of a cultural revolution. It represents first and foremost a sensitive, responsive insight into the meaning of one's own existence in the world and society. His stance coincides with a general tendency which, according to sociologists, characterizes the generation brought up in the mythology of counterculture: a trend that expresses a generational mistrust of all radical attempts to change the existing order[xix] in favor of deriving the sense of our significance from personal experience. It is by way of such experience, in which art brings to light the real humanity of man in the sense we previously described — and only through this experience — that the passage from one's own existence to a socially meaningful situation can be achieved. Firstly a personal work, then a transformation of mind, and finally (but only as a consequence of the first two stages) changes of the world, in the world; in this way Tylicki's attitude is closely related to the political views of Breton. Art is primarily caring about a spiritual quality of life which is taking place in a tumultuous, exciting, but equally overwhelming world; our values, choices, projects, and programs have to grow from a full life experience.

While the concept of play enabled us to create *a*

transition from the reflection on beauty, too narrow to encompass a radically broadened perspective of contemporary art, to our present field of consideration, it also implies a new subject, that is: potential partners in our play. For play is the original experience of community.

.

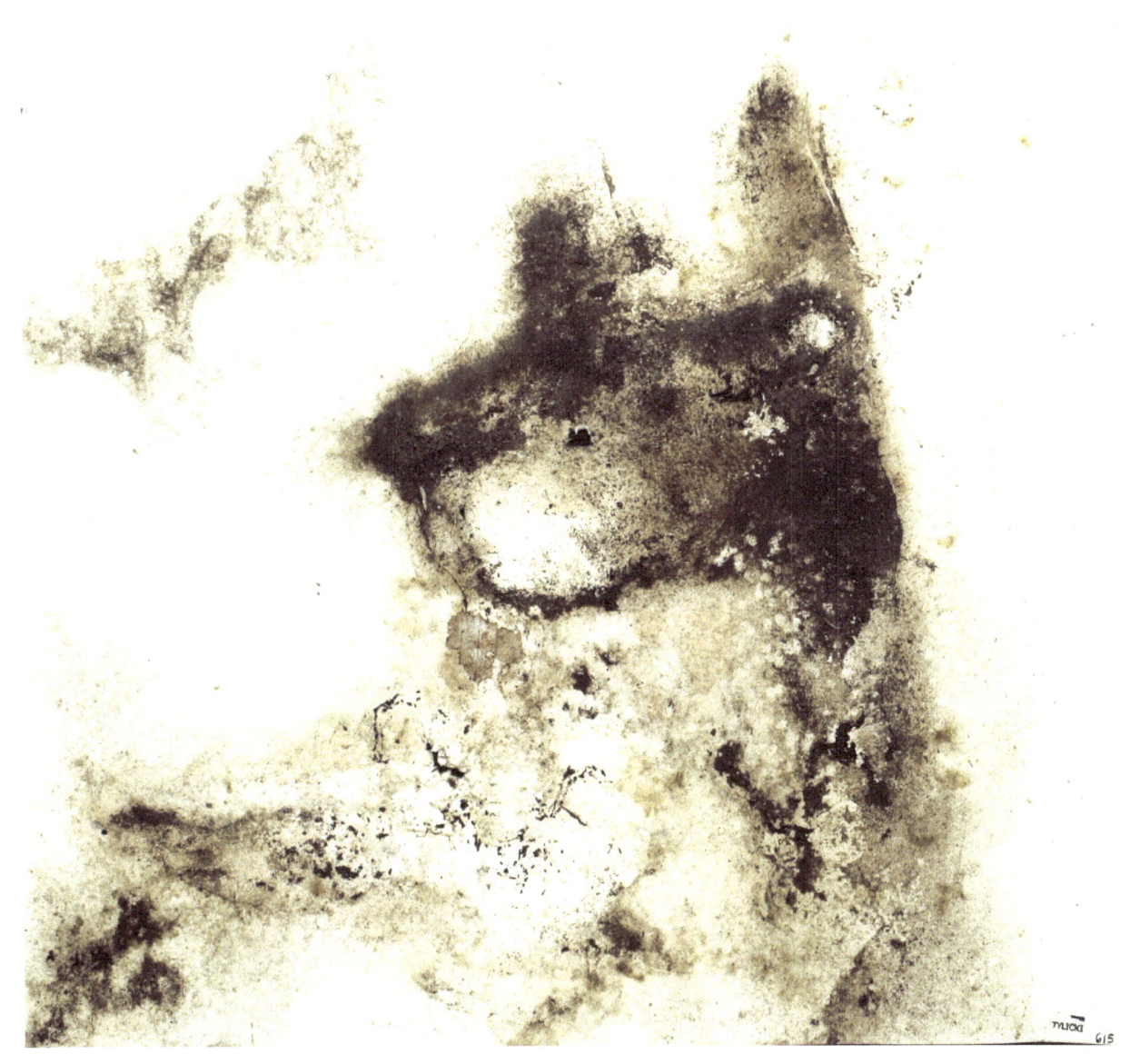

Nature No. 615

On the ground of the forest for 21 days.
Frost Valley, Catskills, USA. May 12 - June 2, 1996
Watercolor paper. 41.9 cm x 38.1 cm

VI.

We asked ourselves: "what is art?" At the beginning we looked for answers in art itself. The idea of art for art's sake channeled us to a conception of art as a perspective defined by the experience of a complete, un-mutilated being, and, in consequence, to a certain type of humanism characteristic of Jacek Tylicki's art. Relying upon this experience we found it possible to look at art as an agreement, a form of common understanding, which creates a foundation for a human community. The road we took to discover the social aspect of art was indirect — it passed through the existential experience. There was a tendency in the seventies, and perhaps even more so in the eighties, to immediately situate art in its social dimension, while at the same time emphasizing that all aesthetic categories are only a matter of convention. With the neophyte eagerness the prevalent philosophy of this period proselytized the social aspects of art and nearly effaced the fact that all creative activity originates in some form of existential experience, which pours meaning into our being by opening us to new, or perhaps only forgotten dimensions, and by bringing back together the divided facets of life and the world. Only one step separates such a superficial — sociological in the most sterile sense — vision of art from the ideology of success or the sociology of domination. We can recall several instances where similar blurring of the values and "hijacking" of critical thinking produced rather questionable results, such as for example the ideology of winners proclaimed by "*Transavanguardia*" ("trans-avant-garde") of Achille Bonito Oliva, a blind pursuit of great commercial success so characteristic of many artists, or the fad for "socially" engaged art, so often practiced by artists otherwise incapable of surviving even the most banal social situation, such as an interaction with friendly neighbors.

Tylicki's art does not "resort" to social experiences. The projects *Make War in Art, not in Reality* [xx] or *Free Art* are directly involved in social interactions. But they are based on his existential *experience*, which *certifies* the meaning and authenticity of all his actions and projects. Tylicki reaches the social dimension of art by virtue of being able to convey his own experience of humanity. Wilhelm Dilthey went even further than Kant or Schiller in emphasizing the point that at the source of every creative activity lies a complete, multidimensional existence, in which concepts, goals and system of values are built into an inherently unified, meaningful structure: "a poet creates with the entirety of his capability[xxi], he wrote. According to Dilthey the humanities had the unyielding obligation to look at man "un-mutilated", unbroken (*unverstümmelt*)[xxii] by conceptual reductionisms of all kinds, empowered by the completeness of his experience and actions.

Inasmuch as war represents one of the hardest and most traumatizing ordeals for humankind, the revolt — even if hopeless but still a voiced one — against the bestialities of the wars that plague our planet, a reaction which we may believe should be natural yet is in fact all but too rare (who keeps a count of one hundred and some thousands of victims of the war in the Persian Gulf?), such a reaction is in fact a work of art in the humanist cause. It is a project for the restoration of a human way to live, and to survive inhuman events. In his own commentary to *Make War in Art...,* Tylicki noted: "I believe it must have been a reaction to the truculence of New York and the world in general that I found very unsettling at the time".

It is only in this context that we can fully appreciate the deep meaning — as well as the unceasing relevance — of the Kantian thesis, according to which aesthetic experience oriented toward engaging other people has to pass through the authentication   of our own humanity. In Tylicki's case this takes place in an act of revolt conceived as a series of artistic activities. Perhaps referring to the memorable slogan of the counterculture "make love, not war" Tylicki looks for inspiration in the counterculture's poetics and logic: we must love instead of killing, but, if war is what you want, you must make it in art. Jacek opened up the doors to his studio "U" on New York's Second Street, where in a huge space his constructions built for the purpose of "aggression", attractive by their total ludicrousness and absurdity, provided a backdrop for hours-long spectacles. The constructions resembled inventive sculptures-mobiles which brought to mind the metamechanics of Tinguely or the Shooting Paintings of Niki de Saint Phalle, and which — to use an expression of Janusz Baldyga — provided the occasion "to use force".

We can think of several thoughts which lie at the origin of this project. By far *Make War in Art...* can be seen as shaped by some of Tylicki's painting ideas. As early as the seventies, when instead of painting canvases Tylicki used to spread sheets of the watercolor paper in a natural environment in order to see the effects produced by nature, the artist extended the process of the "natural" painting into the domain of the "gravitation of paint". His fascination with the finesse and the abundance of the most intricate detail in the patterns created by nature provided an impulse to experiment with another type of natural activity, in which the explosion of paint — falling from the height of several meters then splashing and spattering upon the ground — created in a fraction of a second amazingly detailed and incisive abstract paintings. And while the reverberations of Jackson Pollock's Action Painting seem obvious, we must also observe that the deep nature of the chance factor is very different in Tylicki's work; it is marked by the objectivity of the laws of gravity and the mechanics of the two colliding bodies. We could risk a statement that *Make War in Art...* applies painterly inspirations provided by Pollock's experiences with "dripping" to the field of Natural Art; and it does so by following the principle used by Marcel Duchamp in his "3 Standard Stoppages".

The interest in the gravitation of paint, speed - made into a rule for creating aesthetically complex and varied forms, as well as energy - transformed into form, found their extension a few years later with some early manifestations directly preceding *Making War in Art…* At this time painterly activities are being reinforced with a social aspect, influenced by feelings of rebellion against a world filled with aggression. Not insignificantly, this coincides with Tylicki's leaving essentially pacifist and ecologically minded Sweden and his coming to New York City. From his very first days in New York Tylicki initiates a series of nocturnal "attacks", during which half a gallon glass bottles filled with black paint are being used as Molotov cocktail. The artist begins a long process of taming aggression, or a peculiar project of annihilating aggression by acts of aggression. Tylicki likes to compare this reverse action to the operation Andy Warhol performed with his Brillo Boxes. As in classic guerrilla warfare the attacks are undertaken by groups which must preserve their anonymous character. The original enthrallment with a form of gravity gives way to a reflection upon the ratio between the amount of energy used for an "attack" and the typical shape of a mark left on a derelict wall. A black blot of splattered paint is in itself a signature, and as such — still strictly anonymous — it eventually makes its way to several anthologies of graffiti.[xxiii] (Perhaps the graffiti connection gives Tylicki an idea for Attack in the Fashion Moda Gallery (Attack #3, 1986) ; a place created by Stephen Eins in the South Bronx, which became legendary in the history of graffiti.) The creation of form becomes inseparably related to an "attack", an "attempt" on the integrity of the surface which is about to receive paint. In a certain manner, Jacek's "attacks" shed light on the essence of the relationship between the gesture of an artist and the form created by this gesture, which has been long established in the Western tradition. In contrast to delicate strokes of brush, barely touching the paper in Chinese painting and calligraphy, "in the West", according to Hubert Damisch, "the idea of a line (...) is traditionally, in the first place, linked (...) with a knife that cuts into the surface in order to mark the surface of a plate or a parchment.[xxiv] A certain kind of aggression is therefore embedded in the relation between the artist and the form — Tylicki's attacks try to shift the accent from the form to the nature of this relation.

Finally, there is also an element of risk, which is of course implied by the illegal activities of an illegal alien living in the United States. The risky element, a consequence of an artistic path consciously chosen by Tylicki, represents another type of existential authentication, in which an unavoidable conflict with the American police force appears as a matter of a deep internal need, and motivation behind his art project.

What follows these preliminaries is the project entitled *Make War in Art, not in Reality,* comprised of several installations and actions. Elaborated equipment based on the mechanics of collision and the laws of gravity: bows and arrows, catapults and trapdoors, crossbows and slingshots, containers of paint and pumps, faucets, taps and

safety valves — Tylicki brings all of this to replace nature, up to now his main form-finding element. As with *Natural Art* here also Jacek does not get directly involved in composing the forms; his proxy in this process is machinery, activated by members of the audience. Perhaps the most important point to make here is that in *Make War in Art,...*, the action itself — the play — gives meaning to the whole project.

Throughout this play art symbolically attracts the violence and takes it upon itself in order to diminish — also symbolically — the level of aggression present in the world. We said: "symbolically", because we did agree earlier on that art is a form of playing. However, in the case of war the relationship between play and reality appears to be far more complex. According to Huizinga, in human history wars always contained some elements of play. We can only too well remember the painful astonishment of Native Americans progressively confronting nearly complete extinction (they were, after all, better warriors, capable of setting traps for stupid white men...) — not realizing that in the situation of war the Westerner has a tendency to ignore the distinction between play and reality. We saw the most recent example in the war of the West with Iraq. The difference disappeared earlier for the Futurists, who wanted to see War both as a fascinating spectacle and a way of wiping out the past. Not without bewilderment we read the words of Kant: "even war, if conducted in an orderly way, and with reverence to the rights of the citizens, has something of the sublime about it[xxv].

Jacek Tylicki's attitude toward war leaves no space for ambiguity. There are things that mustn't be trifled with, even if it is otherwise possible to encapsulate them symbolically within a playing — a fact which could lend itself to a four-fold interpretation. First of all, by avoiding the danger of a "War game" Tylicki once more emphasizes the salutary value of playing in human life; a value which in our culture is too often shifted back to childhood and replaced with "adult", dangerous substitutes. Secondly, *Make War in Art, not Reality* offers a prospect of a psychoanalytical cure by creating, in the context of artistic play, the possibility of releasing our repressed aggressive impulses. Thirdly, the project: a series of actions represents an unequivocal protest against war and violence, and ipso facto, a peaceful declaration of art. Finally, it proposes a certain way of making art.

In a commentary, quoted at the opening of this essay, Jacek talks about ways in which society puts restrictions on man's activities in order to reduce him to an element of relatively stable and controlled structures. Society also invents and imposes a certain model of art. According to Walter Benjamin, who wrote extensively on the subject, beginning with the second half of the nineteenth century, our society began to identify the value of art with its monetary power, based on the price that any work of art can fetch on the market, and on its value as an investment, or as a centerpiece on a wall of an executive office.[xxvi] Tylicki's actions are designed to bring chaos to such pseudo-social models of art, to destabilize them by attacking the principle of their foundation. The <u>free</u> distribution of works of well established New York artists (Now Gallery, in a project entitled *Free Art*) puts in doubt not only the capital-value character of an art object, but more than that, the commercial principle of profit, involved in the exchange of commodities. The fundamental attitude of disinterestedness is brought to play in yet another perspective, finding an additional meaning; disinterestedness is now realized in the form of a gift.

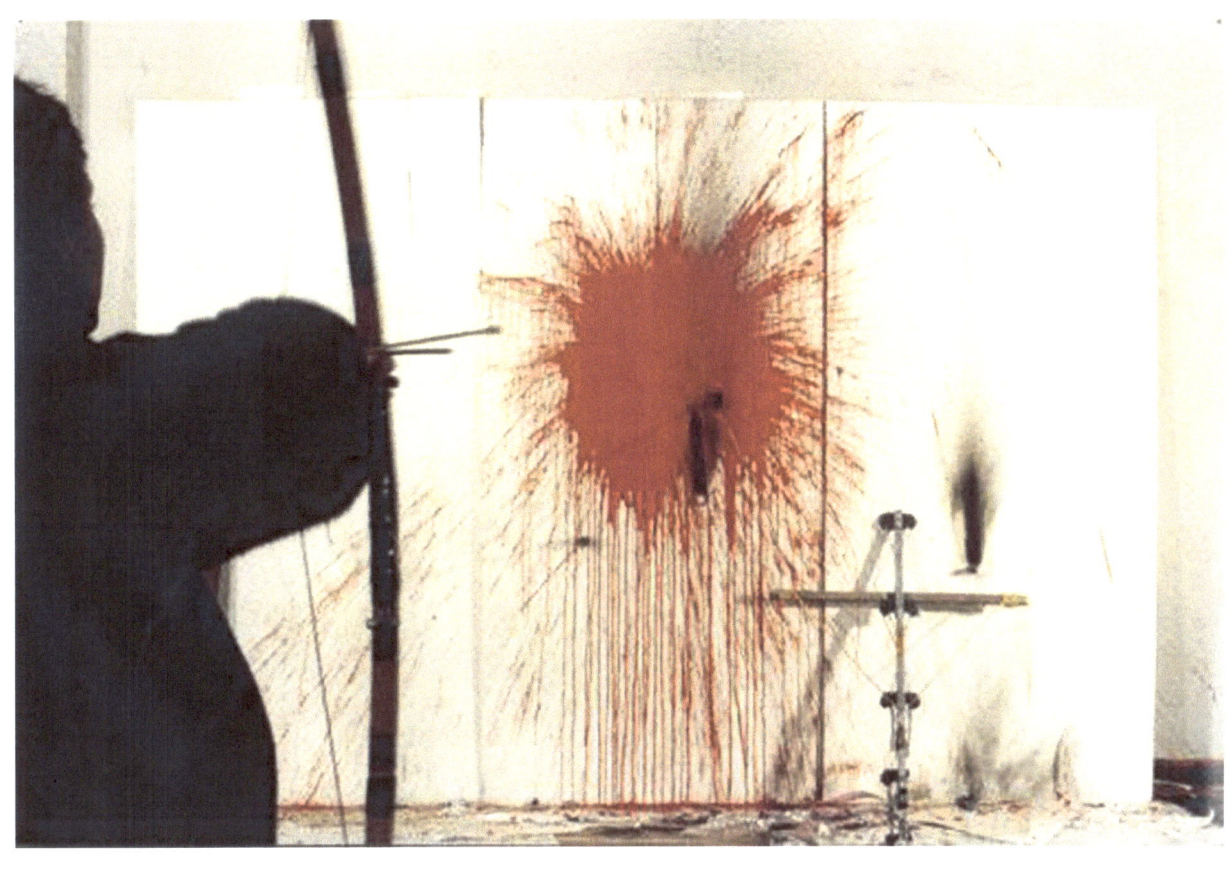

Make War in Art not in Reality

Attack #3
Fashion Moda Gallery, New York 1986

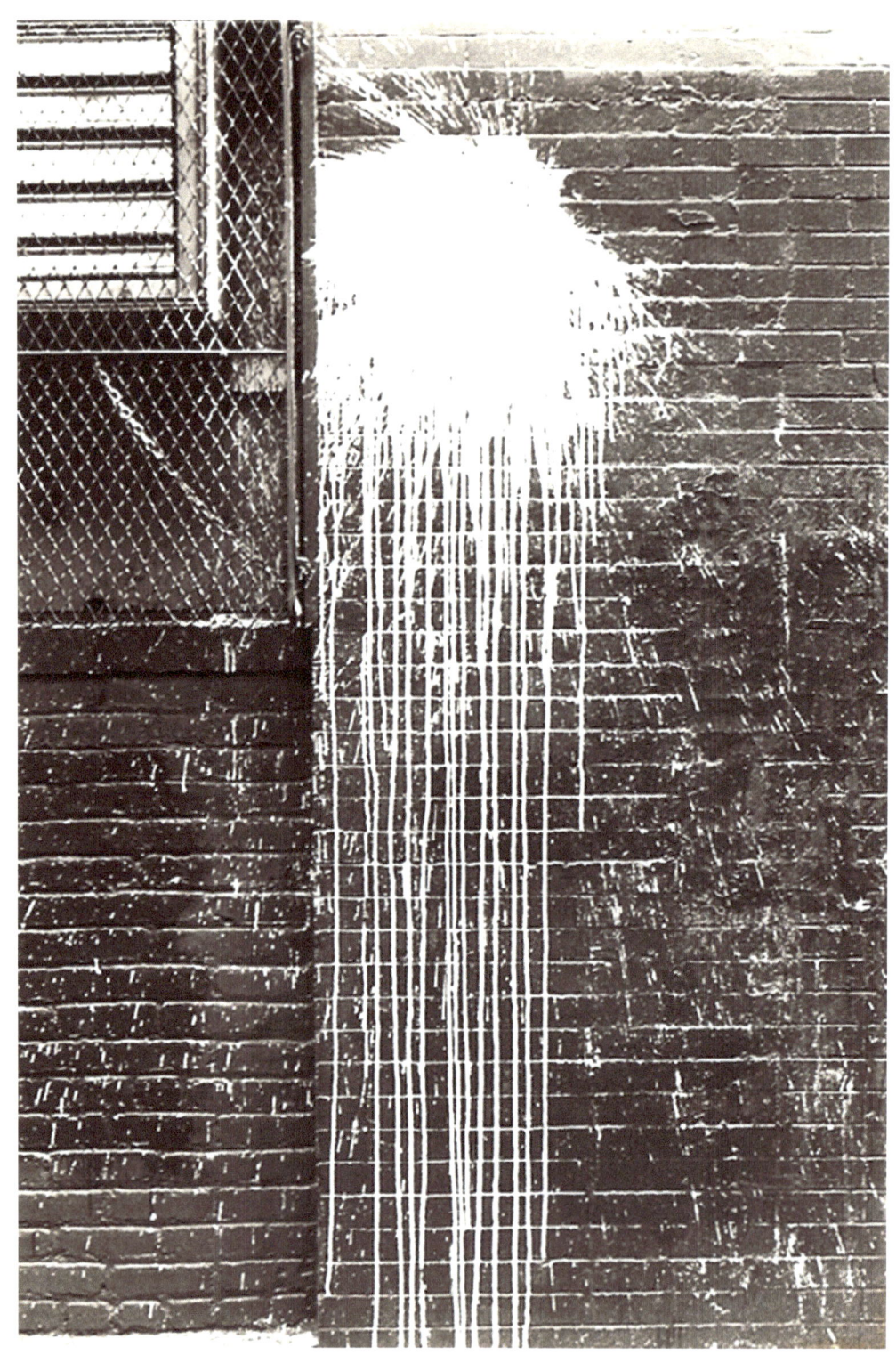

street art wars, New York 1982

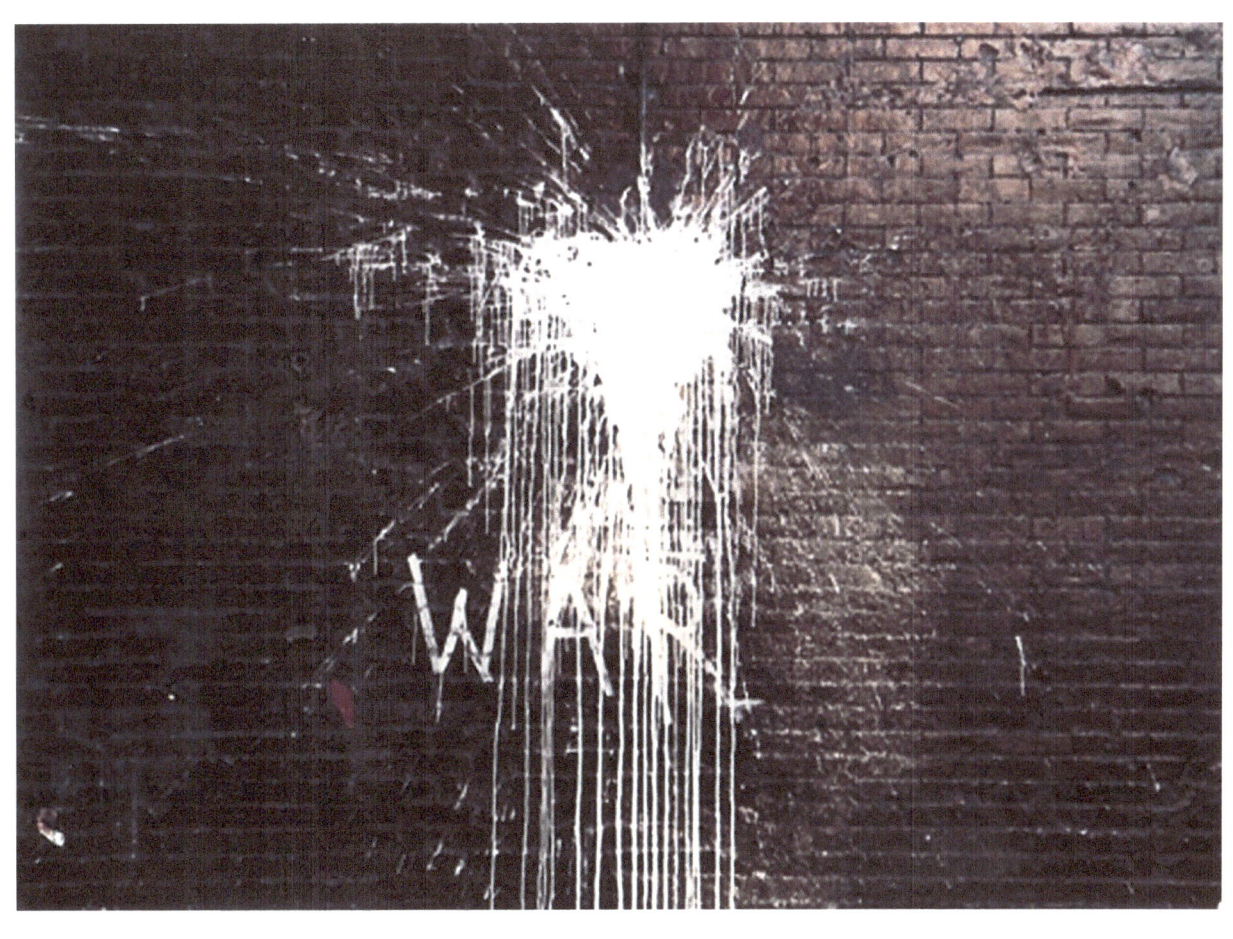

street art wars

East Village, New York 1982

VII.

It is quite a common custom among artists themselves to exchange their works, or to offer them to friends as birthday gifts. Why not then go a step further and make a more general gesture: transform art into a gift, which would open the door to different ways of being in society? The answer seems obvious, if not slightly banal — an artist has to make a living from his art and the way to do it is by selling paintings or taking fees for publishing poems. As we said, this appears to be normal. But *is it* normal?

Free Art of Jacek Tylicki definitely reopens the debate on this subject. Because first of all, we can be absolutely certain that it was not normal for Baudelaire. A romantic poet *par excellence,* catapulted into a modern urban situation with its growing bourgeoisie, Baudelaire felt a huge dissonance in his creative condition. On the one hand he was capable of analyzing, quite cynically, the strategies that a poet like himself must adopt in order to convince publishers and journal editors (*Conseils aux jeunes littérateurs*), but on the other one he could not imagine his own life as an artist as other than on the social margins. Particularly distressful for Baudelaire was his forced flirtation with the bourgeois audience: an artist must sell his poems to survive; however, by doing so he in fact prostitutes himself.[xxvii] If art is important — if in fact it represents one of the most important human values — and if indeed the origins of art lie in the profound experience of our existence then unrestricted attempts to sell it for financial profit must indeed arouse objections.

Jacek approaches this question in a double way. Social habits (which after all stem out of social inertia) can be overturned in order to allow artists to be independent of the sale of his work, making art take place inside economic mechanisms but without the mediation of objects as works of art (*Business as Art*) and at the same time, to free objects of art from the market's encroachment (*Free Art*). Tylicki achieves this goal by opening the door for two possibilities: an independent artist and a liberated art — an art which, depending on its attitude, will then become a game (Business as Art, from 1986 on), or a gift (Free Art).

A liberal rationalist would immediately call us to order: "let us not be naive", he would say, "history has always been a struggle of economic powers. The principle of economic gain is a fundamental factor in organizing social structures. It wouldn't be sensible, or may even be dangerous, to negate its power. Furthermore" — he would add — "the market value of art works appears to be directly proportional to their aesthetic value". These words could in fact represent today's ruling ideology, which organizes the life of the entire planet and to a large extent also the movements of the art market. This self-proclaimed non-ideology, disguised as a sensible view emerging from the time when all ideologies had failed, maintains that everything constitutes a commodity that can be turned into money, therefore art projects must also maintain their monetary value. *Ökonomie über alles!*

Our liberal interlocutor failed to read the fascinating study of Marcel Mauss, published in 1923, "The Gift: forms and functions of exchange in archaic societies" (*Essai sur le don*). Mauss' text, considered today a classic of anthropology, confirmed the ancient knowledge that societies are animated by, and thrive on, the movement of exchange between their constitutive groups. It did not however suggest — which is perhaps the most innovative of Mauss' ideas — that reciprocal exchange has to be reduced to commercial transaction, following the principle of material gain. Examining the reasons that lead a person, or sometimes entire groups of humans, to present someone with a gift, and for others to give something in return, Mauss proved that such an exchange can not be reduced to a commercial activity following the profit principle. The laws of economics do not explain the nature of gifts, because, according to Mauss: "Down deep an exchange consists in a union. Souls are uniting with Things. Things are uniting with Souls. Lives mix so that the individuals and the objects can leave their original space and mix together: that is the contract of an exchange.[xxviii] Not only are material objects subject to exchange; in many cultures people exchange services, dances, rituals, festivities, women, children, and names... "Let us then exchange Art." "Free Art is a challenge: Art can be a gift, Art is a gift, Art as a gift", says Tylicki. Marcel Mauss proved that some forms of social behavior are organized by rules that are contradictory to the economic principle of profit. An alternative principle, which he introduced, is established by the gift.[xxix]

So if the economists neglected to pursue a holistic reflection on the phenomenon of exchange, but reduced it to the principle of economic profit (a fact which elicited Mauss' major objection) then maybe it will fall specifically to Art to initiate such a reflection in a different, creative way — both theoretical and practical — about human exchange.

Jacek Tylicki's *Free Art* was an invitation to such reflection; it would be wonderful if it had started more than just another debate, if it had produced a genuine movement, a tendency, a general levy... We could imagine that an impulse already exists — beginning in the late sixties, the spirit of a voluntary exchange between all artists of good will received a considerable boost from the invention of the world wide web (networks) and Mail Art; it is of course inherent to the production of fanzines, samisdats and artists books. "Artists of good will reunite!"

With the creation of *Free Art*, a project where art takes on, or perhaps returns to, the original form of a gift, Jacek strikes a resonant chord. Art can be offered as a gift in forms other than that of a physical object which we receive. In the exhibition entitled "Largesse" presented in the Louvre in 1994, Jean Starobinski follows the theme of gift in his drawings, texts, and films, with a full awareness that in social situations a gift can also be a source of ambiguities. For example the act of largesse, evoked in the title, symbolically represented by an image of golden coins thrown by handfuls at the coronation of a king (who himself is a symbol of power), turns sour and results in a brawl, because even the most generous gesture can not satisfy greed. While a similar moment of ambiguity slips into the actions of *Free Art* Jacek makes no effort to efface it, but rather provides a lapidary comment: "the audience, which was tipped off by the press release, waited for over 12 hours in front of the gallery to snatch the works of art they longed for..." The purpose of these actions isn't to turn gifting into alms giving, with its humiliating aspect, but to create an opening. Just as Starobinski's exhibition ended with Mallarmé's "A roll of the dice", in which gift is not so much a subject of the poem, but the other way round: it is now the whole poetic world that turns into a gift. The essence of Tylicki's *Free Art* is not the gift as a work of art given by such and such an artist, but a paving of the way for Art's different, utopian circulation in society, and the creation of a new or maybe simply forgotten type of exchange in Art, that could embrace perhaps not only objects, but also thoughts, everyday gestures, games, beauty, events, and maybe even names... precisely, the action known as *Free Art* was organized by Jacek Tylicki as an Anonymous Artist, even though the work given to the audience was produced by known artists. Beginning with the fanzines published in Sweden in the seventies under just that title, Anonymous Artist is a welding material for the whole series of Jacek's projects. The point is precisely to avoid, even to overthrow, a certain egocentrism, connected with the transfer, evident in the modern world, of the emphasis away from the work of an artist onto the artist himself, engendering the phenomenon of "stardom". When Benjamin's "aura" dissipates "we do not admire works of art any more, but artists only[xxx], as Régis Debray — not without reason — remarks. The condition of anonymity means the auto limitation of the author's rights, which represents one of the forms of property rights. Politically speaking it is a refusal of the principle of capitalization of a value attached to the name of the artist; esthetically speaking, it is an attempt to abort one's own greed of owning, and not, as some may suggest, a way of avoiding responsibility for one's work. Quite the contrary: because the focus shifts away from the myth of the artist, the emphasis is placed once more on the essential aspect of creative work. Taking a critical distance from one's own egocentrism is a first step toward art, one which is open to a social network based on the principle of gift, rather than being a commodity. *Free Art*, a project signed by *Anonymous Artist* achieves the creation of an opening: the noble gesture of offering their works as gifts, frequently cultivated by artists, suggests a new possibility for art.

We may pose here to ponder whether or not the critique of a certain aesthetic conception which bound art to its physical object, presented in *Art & Language*, was not in fact too one-sided. In his actions, Tylicki proved that even as a physical object[xxxi], the work of art can be liberated from at least some its determinants (social, legal, economic, etc.) The paradigm of art is constituted not only by the ways of creating the work, but also, and in equal measure, by the ways of its prospective usage, i.e. as a gift, or as a commodity for sale.

In the case of Tylicki's *Free Art*, the gift-aspect clearly nullifies the commodity; the works' monetary value was quite real, amounting to some 30,000 dollars.[xxxii] Furthermore, the cancellation of the economic mechanism reinforces the projection of a new value created by treating art as a gift. In this respect Tylicki reaches further than the Social Art born out of the critical awareness of the conceptualist era. During the seventies, Fred Forest in his outstanding actions derided art speculators and unmasked the utter absurdity of the art market.[xxxiii] Forest's art is an example of a strong, passionate commitment. However, even though "The Artistic Square Meter" and many other of his projects certainly break the social or legal schemes that in a way imprison art[xxxiv], they do not put forward —as it is the case for Tylicki— a program; we can therefore see them as a preparation, rather than an opening. The actions of Fred Forest are meant to clear the ground, to provide critical awareness and to deconstruct. All of Tylicki's work in the field of art — which speaks of his originality and the value of his art — is an attempt to find an ordinary human response to an increasingly dehumanized world, it is a naive magnanimity that opposes a cynicism, a way of nullifying the effects of egoistic greed by disinterestedness, a proposition in the place of a deconstruction, a gift standing against the principle of economic profit.

At this point we must examine our initial (even though slightly prosaic) objection: the entire program will turn into the thin air if the generous artist can't feed himself. This is why we proposed at the beginning of this section to consider *Free Art* in conjunction with another one of Tylicki's project, entitled *Business as Art*.

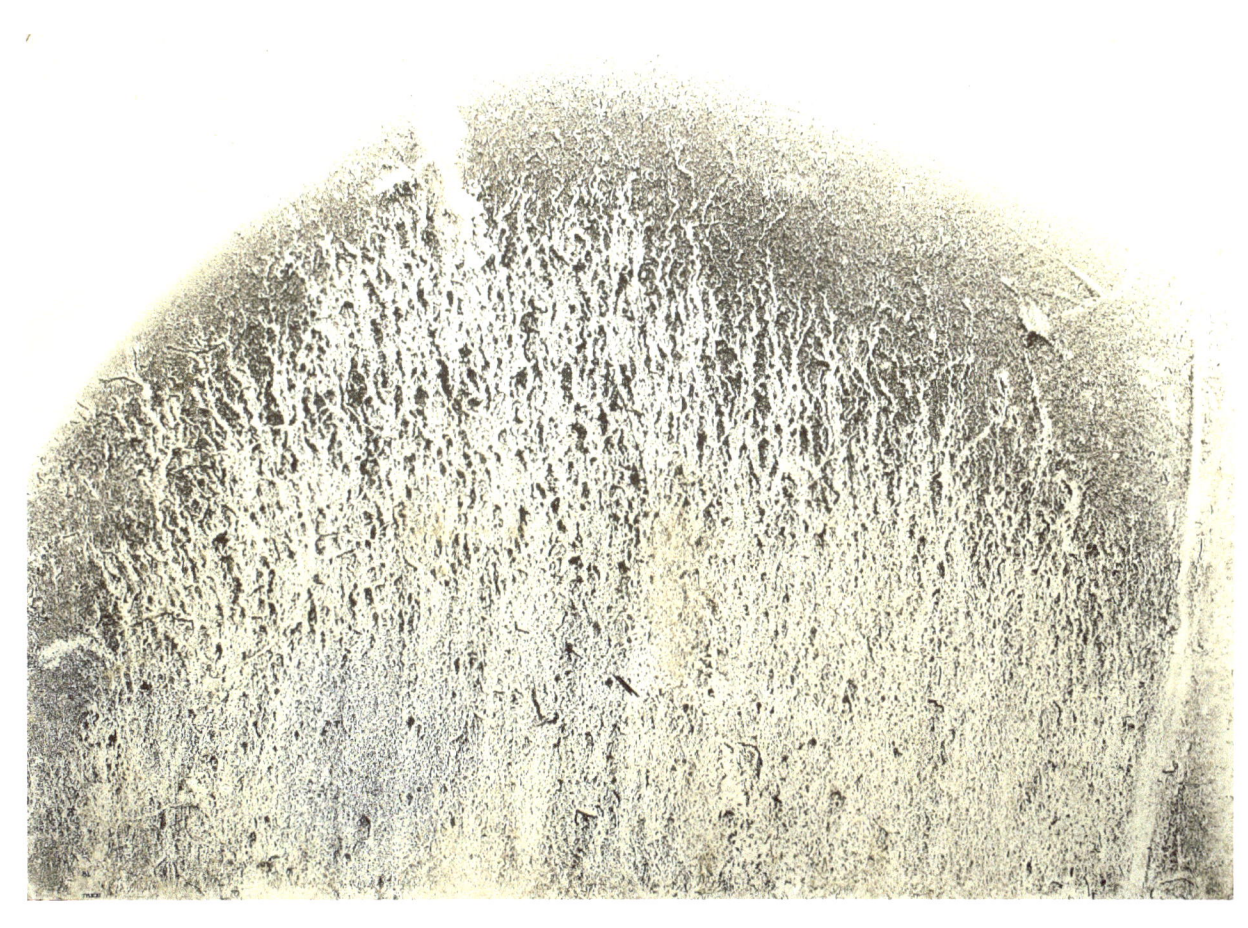

Nature No. 81

3 days on the bank of Höje River.
S.W. of Lund. Sweden.
727 x 507 mm. On museum board.

VIII.

If at first glance *Business as Art* seems like a very provocative idea, it is no doubt because we are immediately confronted with a question which leaves us uneasy: are we witnessing some kind of misuse of art, a manipulative maneuver, meant to revalorize business under the banner of art, but, at the same time, throwing art back into the marketplace and making it play by its rules? (We observe here, at least on the surface, the situation which is the reverse of the one created by *Free Art.*)

Johann Gottlieb Fichte, a great philosopher of action, wrote that: "every man who seeks perfection, will find occasions to perfect himself in every activity.[xxxv] Tylicki's project *Business as Art* is after all an expression of an active approach to the world and, according to Fichte, only a passive attitude stands in opposition to culture. But could it be reconciled with a very specific philosophy of life, such as that projected by Jacek's entire art project, as construed and discussed in his own writings?

The issue of motivation appears to be critical. If the condition of dependence of the artist on the art market has many dire consequences — in times of good markets as well as in those of financial crisis — then Tylicki's attempt to free himself from its grip in order to achieve independence seems logical. With the purpose of self-organizing, self-determining our destiny. To be <u>free</u> means to be able to self-determine one's own goals through action. We can see how the question of motivation brings us immediately into the realm of ethics.

A similar tendency to free art from the market can be observed in many artistic activities; starting with the late sixties one of the main concerns of the conceptual movement was to equip art with safety devices against the manipulation of the markets. From today's perspective we can tell that such efforts were largely in vain, or rather, that no definitive, or perhaps even more importantly, durable, solution were found. Strenuous endeavors to preserve the independence of art must be continuously kept — new ideas must be put to the test. Even then the problem of the actual socio-economic status of the artist in the contemporary world (and more specifically in the present situation and function of art) remains unresolved.[xxxvi] What other options are there? Are we ousting the art dealer to become our own dealers? Are subventions the only acceptable way to go? Or should we indeed consider projects, such as *Business as Art*, which propose extending art —"playing art"— to other, non-artistic domains.

There is of course the question of the nature of the game designed by Jacek. We can perfect ourselves in every possible situation, but could this game really turn into a game of art? We can remember many types of game, which artists of the past used to practice *as art*: the Dadaist Arthur Cravan considered boxing as his artistic discipline, Marcel Duchamp cultivated the game of chess. Contemporary artistic consciousness finds accurate expression in Dlubak's remark that "the structure of art can be realized with many different materials", while Kosuth — as we mentioned earlier on — wants to see the essence of an artwork specifically in play carried out within the meaning system of art. In this context there is no apparent reason to deny *Business as Art* its status as an artistic activity. The only unaddressed question is whether or not we can find the ways to fit it into the framework of the philosophy which permeates Tylicki's earlier projects. As we observed on another occasion, Kosuth curtailed the concept of play to a purely semiotic dimension, while for Tylicki playing stemmed from the experience of a profound completeness of being.

In our opinion a satisfactory alignment can perhaps be theorized from the perspective of art ethics. Especially sensitive to the issue of aesthetic responsibility, Ad Reinhardt wrote: "the artist as businessman is uglier than the businessman as artist.[xxxvii] He would, doubtlessly, approve of Jacek's solution precisely because it allows the artist "to enjoy a complete independence in his creation." Freed from the exigencies of the market, the artist subordinates his art only to internal necessity, which corresponds to the traditional way of defining rational freedom (Spinoza). It is a condition of the autonomy of art. Kandinsky gave this Principle of Inner Need a fundamental role in artistic creation.[xxxviii] The solution to the problem of the status of an artist in contemporary society proposed by Business Art fits into Tylicki's *Weltanschauung* not by virtue of its being play which realizes human completeness, but by virtue of an offer of new conditions which will allow the independence of art. Although, as every form of play, this one too implements a unity of chance and necessity.

Art is a rational attitude and activity in the sense that by its means the artist creates a certain vision of the world, and all his decisions, all choices and actions are designed to formulate as best he can a deeply personal expression of this vision. Art expresses it in its own private language; for Tylicki this includes actions, events, installations, and documents. As we can see art is a language which can't be confined to a purely discursive framework and may therefore need an interpretation. We began our interpretation of Tylicki's work by trying to capture nuances of his most general vision, which gives meaning to his whole art project.

Tylicki's attitude speaks more through his *actions* than through his *works*; the value is located in the activity, liberated from the constraints of the profit principle. It is our culture of superficial effects that elevates this principle to the level of ideology. By putting the emphasis on action rather than on its final product, Tylicki redefines the meaning of aesthetic satisfaction for today's needs by debunking its hedonistic character, and paradoxically tying it to the disinterestedness of the wish for a better world. But is he falling into a trap of altruism, such as was exposed by Nietzsche as a subtle manifestation of the "Will to Power"?[xxxix] It appears that in fact being conscious of the paradox related to the disinterestedness of aesthetic satisfaction — with all of the consequences we discovered while examining the aesthetic ideas of Kant — provides a necessary safeguard. In the philosophy of Tylicki disinterestedness indicates the pursuit of an alliance with nature, a desire to achieve oneness both with nature and himself, while art becomes a ground for experimentation with new social relationships. Disinterestedness does not imply — as in the case of the priests and ascetic sages psychoanalyzed by Nietzsche — social isolation understood as a manifestation of superiority, but on the contrary, it serves the purpose of renewing interpersonal bonds by means of art.

If the above reading of Tylicki's attitude seems acceptable, if the vision of the world which we tried to highlight can indeed provide a valid premise of the actions which he carries out, or a sound justification of his artistic choices, then we can perhaps try to interpret some of his projects *in the light of this vision*. The *Weltanschauung* reflected in his art will provide us with guidelines, which may help us understand the meaning of such projects as *Chicken & Art*, *Reconstruction Attempt of the Korpfulsstadir Quarry[xl]*, and the whole series of actions under the common banner of *Anonymous Artist*.

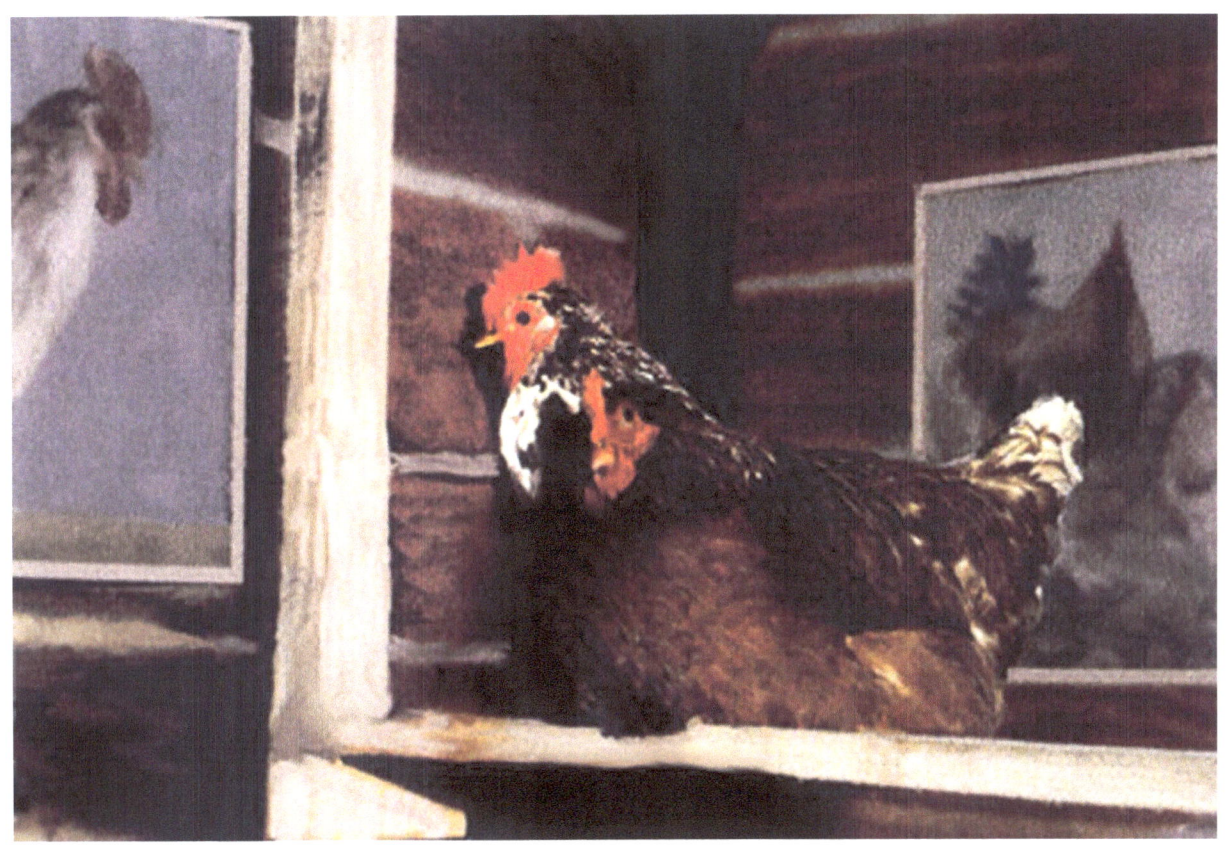

"For a chicken the most beautiful is chicken"

Chicken & Art - NOW Gallery - New York 1987

IX.

"For a chicken chicken is the most beautiful", declares Tylicki with his understated sense of humor, and gives the following commentary on the project entitled *Chicken & Art*: "The gallery was transformed into a henhouse full of live hens and chickens sitting around. On the walls there are a dozen of realistic paintings (created with the help of a group of young New York artists), which, to my mind, ought to please the chickens.[xli] How — other than as a practical joke — could we interpret this gesture? Is this a metaphor for egocentric human relationships, or a disagreement with an exaggerated and misunderstood universalism, which, disregarding Nature, projects its own, devastating order? Both interpretations seem plausible. "The main motive for the realization of this thought" — writes Tylicki — "was probably my irritation with the exaggeration of the beauty of the human body". Or, in other words, individual and genetic narcissism.

For a chicken chicken is the most beautiful; certainly. In a fly-world, one can only find things for flies, (wrote J. von Uexkll in *Umwelt und Innerwelt* in 1909) in a bear-world, only things for bears. Nonetheless, we have to sharpen our question now: is the most beautiful thing for a hen indeed *a portrait* of a hen? For Jacek has created a situation in which hens can observe and admire one another, but at the same time he obliged them to contemplate the beauty of "handsome roosters, beautiful hens and pretty young chickens". Painting is here a locus of an essential transposition, which if we make appeal to Kant's argumentation would have us presume that the beauty of these paintings will not be communicable between hens. Therefore, though at first glance one might believe that the essential intention of the installation *Chicken & Art* was to scoff at "anthropocentric" abuses of universalism, we now come to understand that the question of universalism is much more complicated than that, for the project itself imposes on hens an aesthetic model built on painting. A hen may feel positive excitement at the sight of a rooster, even if it manages to recognize it as such in a painting, but it won't come up with arguments to justify the painting as a model of art, and therefore, the beauty of paintings will remain utterly inaccessible to a chicken.

Only now can we raise the question of universalism (and its inverse, parochialism) and reflect on the relation of beauty to this problem. Tylicki himself realizes that in doing so a question is raised about the "general essence of Beauty. Where is Beauty? What is beautiful, what is ugly? And who for?" From the above questions he comes to a hypothesis, adding however that, "probably: for a chicken chicken is the most beautiful". Certainly. Nonetheless, the artists who portrayed chickens with Tylicki also became very moved by the hens' beauty. Indeed, only a human is capable of having a universal view, rising somehow above local particularities; only a human can take into consideration different points of view. This is universalism, to which the totalitarian tendency of imposing one particular model of culture as a predominantly compulsory reference is foreign. A chicken however is condemned to its "aesthetic" parochialism, which it will never be able to overcome. That is why, set against this, we arrive at a hypothesis, complementary to the one forwarded by Jacek: a hen is not sensitive to human beauty, but only to the "chuck-chuck" of a farmer and the "squawk" of a rooster. But what Beauty is is merely the sublimated vehicle for the libido, for a human, as well as a hen (on condition, however, that one can talk meaningfully about Beauty in the chicken's world). Perhaps behind the apparent disinterestedness of aesthetic satisfaction lie misdirected, and therefore not fully conscious, dark powers, such as the erotic drive (or driving off...), a Nietzschean affirmation of the will to power, or a psychoanalytical mechanism of substitutional realization. The answer can be found among the arguments of *Anti-Oedipus*. In their brilliant psychoanalysis of Psychoanalysis, Gilles Deleuze and Félix Guattari in fact drew attention to the ideological aspect of psychoanalytic theory itself. Their criticism of restrictive culture showed that it served precisely as a pretext for liberal ideology, free-market capital and the law of survival of the fittest. In a sense, a psychoanalytical unmasking of disinterestedness, which is such an important point for the aesthetics of Kant, and which psychoanalysis "suspects" of an erotic "interest" (or, otherwise put, the psychoanalytical thesis of a libidinal foundation of any creative activity) goes hand in hand with the principle of free profit in a field of liberal economy.[xlii]

And if we refuse to accept the profit principle, regarding it as unjustified, groundless, or even inadmissible in a matter of art, not to mention human relations, then we have to consequently keep a distance from any psychoanalytical suspicions of hidden eroticism and the unconscious "will to power" in all attempts at invoking disinterestedness. For it is not without reason that the French philosopher Alain called psychoanalysis "monkey psychology". Disinterestedness seems to be something utterly naive and ridiculous in these times, when charity has become a business, and the libido has ceased to be a taboo to such a degree that — if we were to believe the endless TV commercials seen daily by billions of people around the globe — the only way to fully appreciate a tasty yogurt these days is by acquiring the shape of a gorgeous and entirely naked young woman. "The main motive for the realization of this thought" — says Tylicki about his *Chicken & Art*— "was probably my irritation with the exaggeration of the beauty of the human body and the unceasing trying on of new forms, which turn again and again around the same subject". To be precise: the subject of the "chicken's ass".

The motives of the artistic choices of Jacek Tylicki come together in a formidably consequential way around a certain conception of disinterestedness. This convergence establishes the coherence of his *Weltanschauung*, which he constructs by means of the language of his art. An attempt to replace, in *Free Art*, the economic principle of profit by that of the gift, found its complement and at the same time a continuation of the reflections of *Chicken & Art*, by revealing its intention to separate Beauty from the erotic interpretation to which it was condemned by Psychoanalysis, and to try to show its more universal meaning. For the libidinal dimension of Beauty proved to be an element of the same free-competition ideology of money, which Jacek deprecates in many different ways in his other projects.

Art such as that being practiced by Tylicki is Applied Philosophy, is philosophising by means of objects, events, actions, photographs, etc.; it is a philosophy made manifest as the reality of Art; that is probably why Jacek himself happily speaks of the idea as being the essence of art. Our commentary can only underline the meanings, which although partially hidden, are already implicitly present in the work. If we can succeed in making them stand out — an achievement which every art critic can secretly hope for — it is clear that interpretation can not replace art itself, because art is related to a certain existential attestation, the sense of which we now could try to specify a little more precisely, since we have made it clear that the practice of disinterestedness, in a world ruled by the principle of profit and accepting a liberation of the sexual drive as a condition of freedom, carries with it a certain risk of becoming a laughing-stock. Facing this fear of making oneself ridiculous expresses a fidelity to certain values, for a

dis-interest-ed interest in the beauty of hens, and in beauty for hens, expresses a more general attitude, which betokens a return to the interest of art — although on a new basis — in Nature.

X.

The reason we can talk of a "return" is because a little more than half a century ago, on the grounds of the philosophical thinking of Arthur Schopenhauer, aesthetics made a final attempt to derive the concept of artistic experience from the aesthetic contemplation of nature; the need for art, according to Schopenhauer, is a result of the poverty and mediocrity of the way in which an ordinary person experiences nature. A plain man has no means to grasp aesthetic ideas directly from nature. After Schopenhauer, aesthetics followed the lead of Hegel by putting aside its interest in nature and converging, willy-nilly, in this neutral or perhaps even hostile attitude towards art, with a Cartesian ideology of man as "a master and possessor [*maître et possesseur*] of nature". Such an aesthetically negative relationship to nature will reach its pinnacle in the aestheticism of the *fin-de-siècle*. Baudelaire hated the countryside; Goncourts see nature as their enemy; Whistler and Wilde talk of nature in a tone of sarcastic disdain.[xliii] Huysmans shows an interest in nature only inasmuch as he gets the impression that some of its manifestations follow the ideal of artificiality.[xliv]

Interest in the beauty of nature betokens a disinterested but open and friendly attitude towards it; Tylicki at least does not seek from his experience of nature any cheap, banal or egoistic thrills, but uses it as a springboard for reflecting upon the universality of beauty and the ways we can communicate it. Universality is now colored with yet another message, which is based on the opposition to the relationship with nature, which, starting with Aristotle, has become characteristic of the entire Western tradition. A disinterested approach to nature is the reverse of the ideology of struggle against nature, organized in the name of a certain vision of human work, technology and progress. The role of nature in this vision is at best reduced to something like a raw material; while in the worst case, it is treated as an enemy which man needs to subdue. Insofar as powerful modern technologies are used on an unprecedented, planetary scale, the risks involved in such an attitude impel us to look for a new, "partnership"-style relation with nature, and to develop new technologies based on an alliance with nature, rather than on its subjugation.

The art of Jacek Tylicki tries to meet nature on these freshly re-defined terms. A beautiful, symbolic, alliance with nature was reached through a project entitled *Natural Art*, which granted nature complete autonomy in the process of "painting" pictures, and by doing so, included nature in the creative process. *Living in the Tree* anchors the symbol of the artist's alliance with nature in an experience, during which culture is temporarily (and of course metaphorically) placed in parenthesis. This deeply personal experience of allowing oneself to be completely dependent on one's own nature-skills for a period of time distinguishes Tylicki's action from a naive Primitivism, typical of the first stage of Expressionism. Jacek's initial intention of simply actualizing the oridinary relation with nature gradually gives place to fidelity to "his tree"; a tree in which the artist spent several days, and which subsequently became the subject of a year-long photographic study. Day after day, Jacek returned to the tree to make its portrait.

Another mode of reconciliation with nature represents the *Reconstruction Attempt of the Korpfulsstadir Quarry*. In a gesture of ecological reflection Tylicki examines the relation between destruction and reconstruction. Destruction of nature is very easy; in fact the facility with which we carry out acts of destruction is frightening. It takes seconds to dynamite a rock. However, the reconstruction of the structure that has been destroyed proves almost impossible, because of the incredible intricacies and the subtle complexity of nature's original construction. Things look similar if we consider the ecological balance which by now has been universally threatened throughout our planet — the process of restoring lost equilibrium is going to be lengthy, and its secrets are known only to nature itself. Blowing up a rock does not constitute a de-construction but a de-struction, i.e. a violation of an organic structure; therefore its reconstruction can be seen as a meditation upon the fragility of a rock.

By meditation we mean more than an intellectual reflection; it must encompass and deeply engage the whole being of the artist. Hours spent on the effort to fit a piece of rock, blown up by the explosion, back into its original pocket in the rock's face, produce no distinguishable visual effect. On the other hand, the experience gives the artist an acute sense of the dimensions of the cosmic catastrophe which is provoked by everyday activities of the Western man. A similar type of meditation appears in many different projects of Tylicki, for instance in his 592-point graffito realized in New York City. A leading idea in this case was to "put a maximum of work into what appears to be a "nil" of aesthetic effect." *The Reconstruction Attempt...,* focuses body and soul in a contemplation of the fragility of nature.

It is possible to imagine that Tylicki introduces here a correction to Bakunin's thesis, which proclaims the creative force of destruction, or, to be more precise, reveals its limitations. Lucio Fontana's razor-slashes of painting canvases no doubt represented an act of creative destruction; an open gash in the surface of a painting subjected to aggression adds a whole new meaning to the work. But a gaping crack in the landscape, resulting from man turning his aggression on nature, is only a testimony to our war on nature, tearing its living tissue. In the era of universal destruction and deconstruction, Jacek's attempts to reconstruct provide a valuable counter-proposal. Inasmuch as the New Humanism emphasizes the value of a fundamentally changed relation of man with nature, Tylicki's *Reconstruction Attempt* ..., can be seen as an introduction to this new paradigm; while it has not yet reached the stage of a perfect union between man and nature, it nonetheless constitutes the first step on the path to such an alliance, which mirrors the unity and integrity within nature itself.

In many of his projects, Jacek Tylicki shows that art can be a bridge to nature; crossing it by means of meditation, the artist deepens his newly found experience of being one with nature; and in a further perspective, he discovers a cosmic consciousness of self-identity equal to the identity of the universe to which he belongs. The self-identification with the surrounding world means an overcoming of the ego by way of merging with nature in all its anonymity. "When one brush stroke becomes a measure, the participation in the metamorphosis of the world becomes a reality[xlv], says Shi T"ao, a seventeenth century painter from the Tsing period. "It is unacceptable", wrote André Breton, "that man's presence on the Earth should leave any footprints".

We are interested in finding an answer to the question of whether or not Tylicki's reflection can be read in harmony with this line of thinking.

XI.

Anonymous Artist begins with the fanzines published by Tylicki in Lund (Sweden) in the late seventies under just that title. The idea was simple: to produce a document, which contains no names and no dates; in other words, art only. It is easy to guess that the main concept of the project was born out of the rejection of a certain mythology of the artist whose blessed presence in the universe of mass media is supposed to compensate for the lack of talent. Whatever can be said of the determinants of the social significance attributed to artworks, which is measured by their circulation within the official structures of the art world, the work remains the only true test of the artist's value. The winner is not the one who comes in first: art is not a form of sport. Nor is it the one who's most publicized by the media: an artist is not a Hollywood celebrity. Each and every one of the art networks goes back to an original artistic proposition. Tylicki's response to an exaggeration of the role played by the various mechanisms of promotion of art and artists found its best formulation in the concept of *Anonymous Artist*. Let us imagine an interesting art project, one which has the potential of becoming a source of deep reflection and satisfaction with integrative power; does it really matter (beyond the most obvious level) whether its author is a famous artist, or a student of an art academy? Many of us would agree that it is of little importance, yet nothing attracts more attention than "big names". At times, artistic criteria can be shadowed by certain elements (other than economic), such as the expression of modern mythologies which correspond to our projections of subconscious desires, or marketing mechanisms. The adoption of an anonymous version of artistic creation — which in our time can only be done by free choice — is another attempt to bring us back to the center of the work of art.

Having put out a few issues of the fanzine, Tylicki began to use the title *Anonymous Artist* as a kind of pseudonym and many of his projects, among which *Chicken & Art*, *Free Art*, the "attacks", *Make War in Art...*, etc., were presented in a condition of anonymity.

Of course a whole series of questions and doubts immediately spring to mind. Is there an anonymity beyond one which can be achieved by merging with and disappearing in a large crowd, devoid of personality or expression? Is the artist's name really without significance here, given that the meaning of each work depends in great measure both on the *Weltanshauung* which it expresses along with other projects by the same author, and the exact place it occupies within his entire career path? And finally the most important qualm: that so far we only defined Tylicki's philosophy in the perspective of a specific type of existential experience. For Jacek, a personal testimony of authentic Being-in-the-World — or the Heideggerian Dasein — provides a counterweight to the anonymous authority of science. But doesn't the choice of an anonymous mode of creation reduce, at least to some extent, the importance of personal experience, and by the same token, put a shadow over its authenticity? Can an artist who decides to adopt this ethos of art remain anonymous?

We mustn't forget that the original intention behind this project was precisely to lay stress upon the authenticity of personal experience, which brings forth its value and meaning regardless of the name, which attaches to artwork. This is the way in which *Anonymous Artist* collaborates in the creation of a certain vision of the world, which becomes a horizon of Jacek's art. It is obvious that Tylicki's quest for anonymity does not take him, to quote one example, in a direction akin to the classical Chinese tradition, in which a painter literarily "dissolves", losing himself in an endless and exact repetition of patterns set by centuries of artistic practice. On the other hand, Tylicki's art fits perfectly into the paradigm of rebellion, and frequently has in its conception a rejection of socially sanctioned patterns of behavior. This art exudes a critical attitude towards Western society and its traditions, which means that such an attitude has to be considered a permanent background to Tylicki's projects, and only in such a context can they acquire their full meaning.

In reality two apparently opposed poles — two tendencies of contemporary hermeneutics mark Tylicki's attitude. On the one hand, we have to recognize that the meaning of a work of art functions in a way which is independent of its creator. Any attempt at interpretation must therefore seek to capture this *meaning*, and not the intentions or feelings which the artist wished to embody and project. The days when an artist's work was seen from the angle of his biography appear to be over, and a biographical interpretation is no longer considered to be a valid theoretical conception. In so far as we allow ourselves to frame things in terms derived from Tylicki's own actions, we could speak of the *anonymity* of the meaning, instead of the "death of the author", knowing that the latter idea, which originated in the space between Modernism and Postmodernism, can be controversial. Whereas a parenthetical approach to the artist's biography or name can be perceived as a procedure used to objectify the sense of the work, his experience —which does not directly invade the meaning— nonetheless bears witness to the authenticity of the work. On the other hand therefore, hermeneutics takes an interest in the life of an artist inasmuch as it constantly provides an "ontological authentication[xlvi] of artistic truth. The paradoxical nature of the convergence of these two tendencies lies in the fact that the anonymity of meaning and the "neutralizing" of the artist's name makes the ontological authentication necessary in situations where the prestige of the author was too often taken for granted. Anonymity of meaning pushes the work of interpretation over the brink, in search of the new depth and seriousness that it deserves. From the viewer's perspective, art is rooted in the experience of the interpretation of meaning, while for the artist it is a continuous work of self-improvement, and a field of a personal experience.

At a certain point the idea of *Anonymous Artist* begins

to function as a pseudonym. One may say that the utility of using it reaches its limit when the artist's individual signature gets identified as *Anonymous Artist*. At that moment there is no longer a difference between the artist's real name and the pseudonym he uses. What's left however is a purely symbolic gesture. A pseudonym plays a role of the manifesto, indeed a symbol, which points to the discrepancy between an authentic deep involvement, "lived" through a personal experience, and a turning of the name of an artist into a form of capital.

After the "unmasking" of his anonymity, Tylicki upon finding himself being greeted by friends and strangers as an "anonymous artist", decides to return to his original fanzines. Ten issues of *Anonymous Artists* have come out to this date, but the project remains open and Jacek plans to produce a book of the collected materials; needless to say, the title of the future book is also *Anonymous Artist*.

XII.

Not to give in to the stupefying tempo of the modern world (*Living in the Tree*). To free oneself from pressures of social models of success and owning (*Free Art*). To reject defeatism (*Business as Art*). And to overcome an anaesthetizing effect of the egoism (*Anonymous Artist*). Or, on the contrary, to live in the present but believe in the future (*Make War in Art...,*). Or to think of nature (*Natural Art*) and consider taking time out for a hike in the mountains (*Clock without Hands*). Or be able to afford a disinterested gesture (*Reconstruction Attempt...*). And to learn anew how to dream (*Chicken Art*): all of the above projects add up to a coherent vision, which is an expression of a certain stance, an attitude towards the world, other people, and one's own existence, which man endows with meaning. Only history can give man a good sense of his own identity but in today's world many of us have the unfortunate impression that history reveals a limit beyond which, instead of experiencing humanity, we intuit a terrifying ghost of <u>total</u> self-destruction. As we discussed earlier in this text, reconstruction is the most difficult of all "-structions". A new humanist approach becomes an attempt to save the humanity of a human being — in a human being; it is an attempt to preserve a way of living, feeling, experiencing oneself and the other, of being in the world, which still feels natural, but which from the angle of the mutations of our civilization must appear old-fashioned and out of date.

Another project entitled *Clock without Hands* was realized by Jacek in 1980 on the top of the mountain Esja in Island. As in Ingmar Bergman's film "Wild Strawberries", a clock without hands evokes a symbolic return to the time of our childhood, creates a metaphor of time, which came to a pause at the peak of a childhood reverie. ""By certain of its traits childhood *lasts all through life*." — wrote Gaston Bachelard — "It returns to animate broad sections of adult life. First, childhood never leaves its nocturnal retreats. Within us, a child sometimes comes to watch over us in our sleep. But in waking life itself, when reverie works on our history, the childhood which is within us brings us its benefits. One needs, and sometimes it is very good, to live with the child which he has been. From such living he achieves a consciousness of roots, and the entire tree of his being takes comfort from it.[xlvii]

In her interesting study "Ethos of New Art" ("*Etos Nowej Sztuki*", Warsaw, 1984), Jolanta Brach-Czaina seeks to define the above ethos by taking into account various analyses of art projects of Grotowski, known as *Living Theater*, and the writing of Stachura, and comparing them with the nineteen seventies' trends in the fields of philosophy, sociology, and psychology, such as these trends became apparent in contemporary community-oriented movements, and in medical, as well as economic fashions. In reality, Jacek Tylicki's *Weltanschauung* in many aspects converges with the "ethos of New Art": it lays a stress upon the value of a personal experience as bearing witness to artistic truth, searches, on his own account, for authenticity and fullness of existence, and maintains a critical skepticism toward the ethical models of Western society. To this brief characterization we must also add certain other qualities, which bespeak the originality of Tylicki's path, and bear the mark of our times: an ecological sensitivity; interactions into the mechanisms of social life, which give his art a political meaning; and last but not least, a strong emphasis on certain kind of aesthetic disinterestedness, which becomes a focal point for many of his artistic endeavors, and points us in a direction where we can find the experience of a certain quality of being, one long forgotten or deeply neglected in our culture.

translated by Dorota Czerner

PLATES

Selected from
Catalogue Raisonné
Natural Art series
1973 – 2014

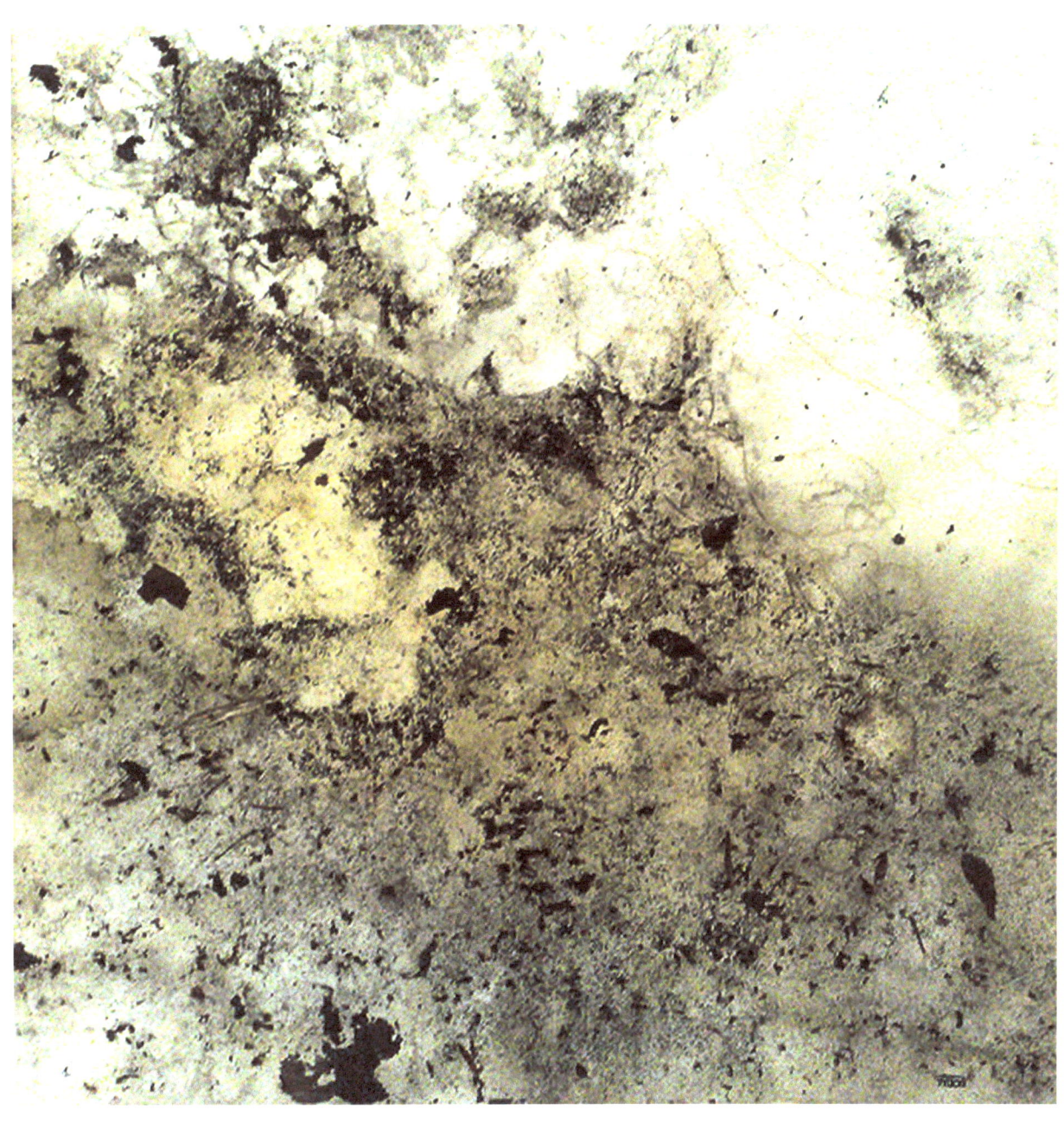

Nature No. 1

In the grass of a meadow.
S.W. of Lund. Sweden. July 16 – 20, 1973
460 mm x 460 mm. Watercolor paper.

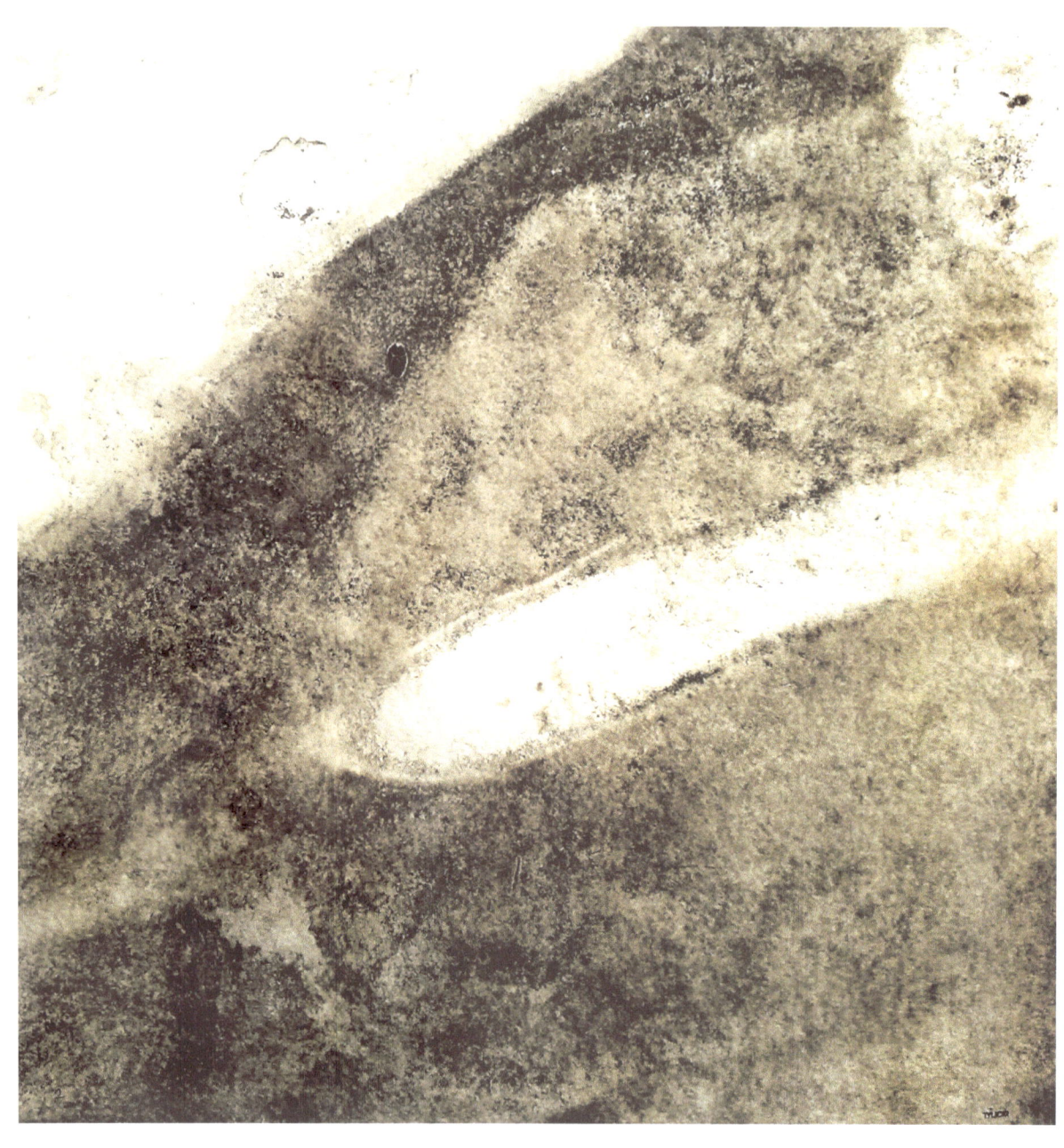

Nature No. 2

On the meadow near Höje River.
S.W. of Lund. Sweden. July 17 – 29, 1973
470 mm x 470 mm. Watercolor paper.

Nature No. 4

On the bank of Höje River.
S.W. of Lund. Sweden. August 8 – 23, 1973
470 mm x 475 mm. Watercolor paper.

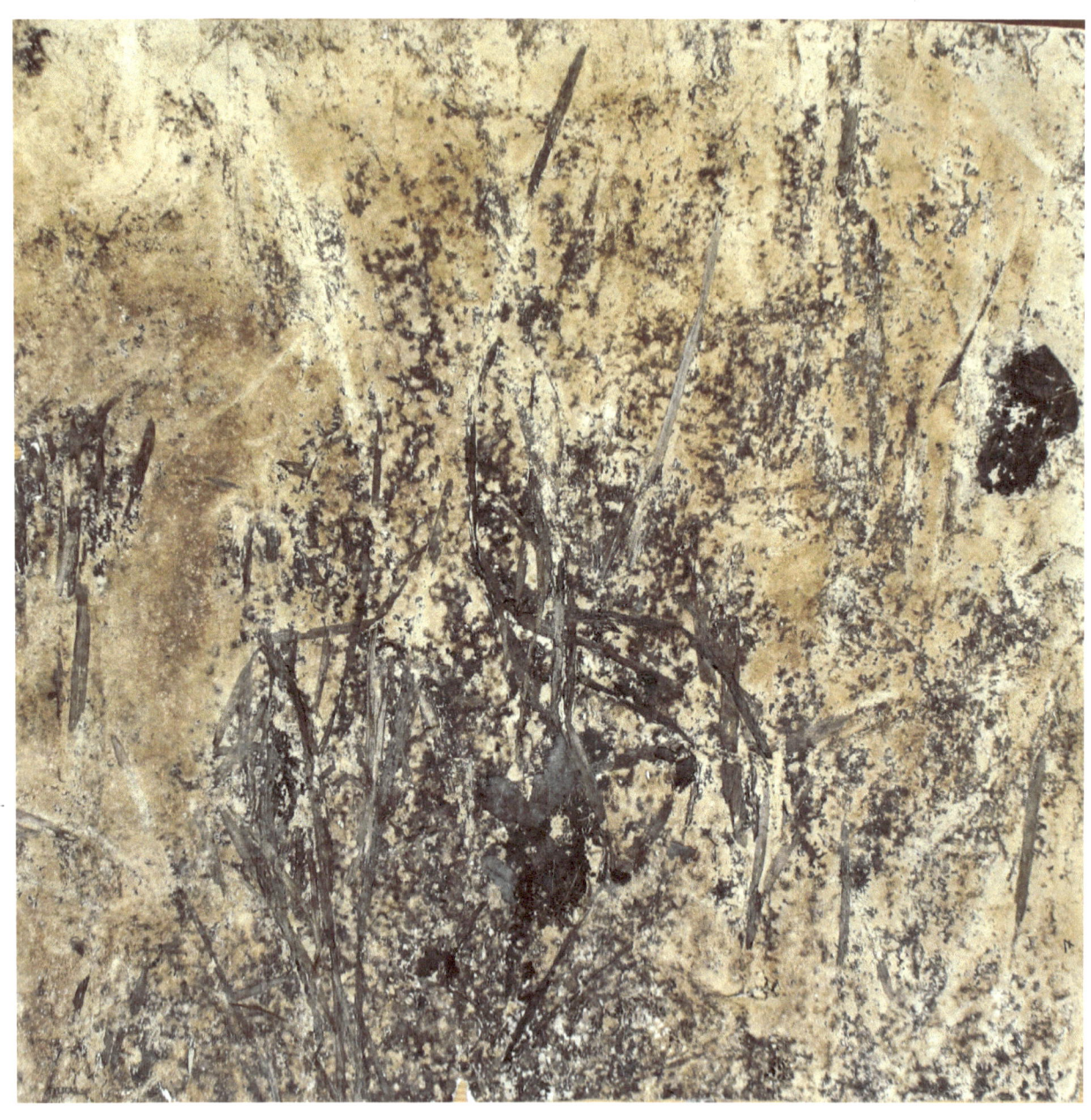

Nature No. 7

Winter in the woods. Dalby Beechwood Forest.
South Sweden. Nov 25 1973 – March 10, 1974
410 mm x 410 mm. Watercolor paper.

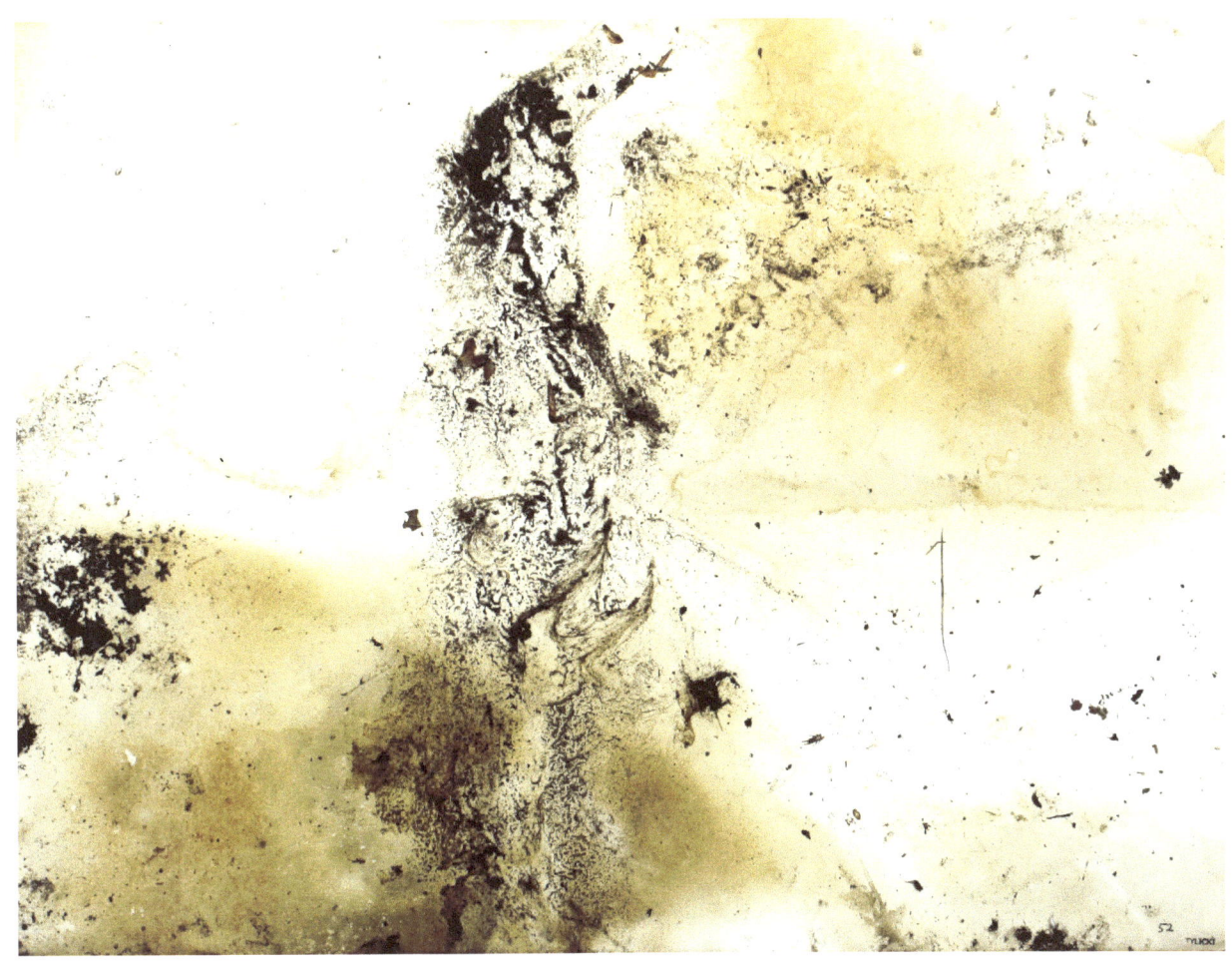

Nature No. 52

On the forest floor. Dalby Beechwood Forest.
South Sweden. Apr 6 – May 23, 1978
475 mm x 355 mm. Watercolor paper.

Nature No. 86

On the bank of Höje River.
S.W. of Lund. Sweden. June 17 – 23, 1978
473 mm x 354 mm. Watercolor paper.

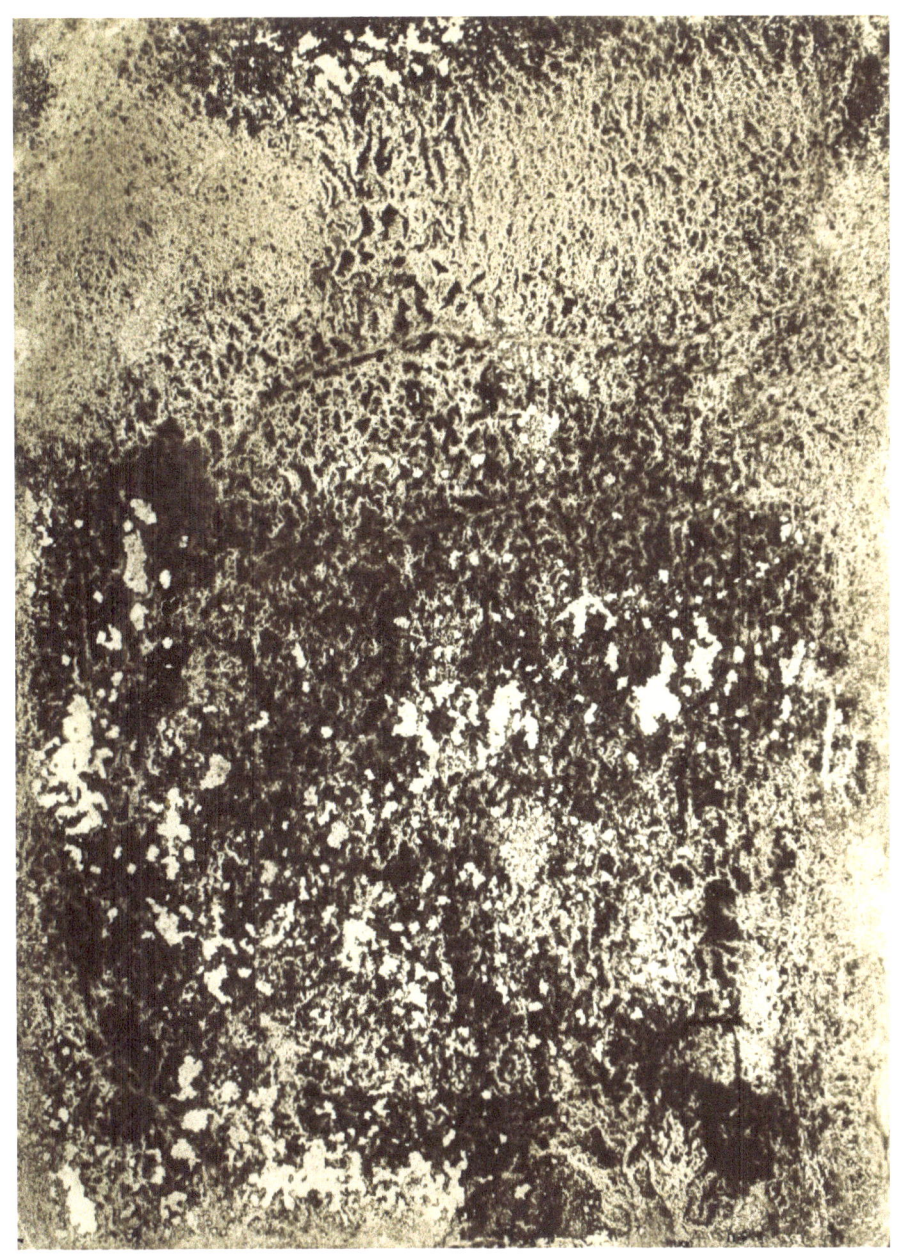

Nature No. 116

On sandy forest floor. Dalby Beechwood Forest.
South Sweden. June 8 – Aug 6, 1978
475 mm x 355 mm. Watercolor paper.

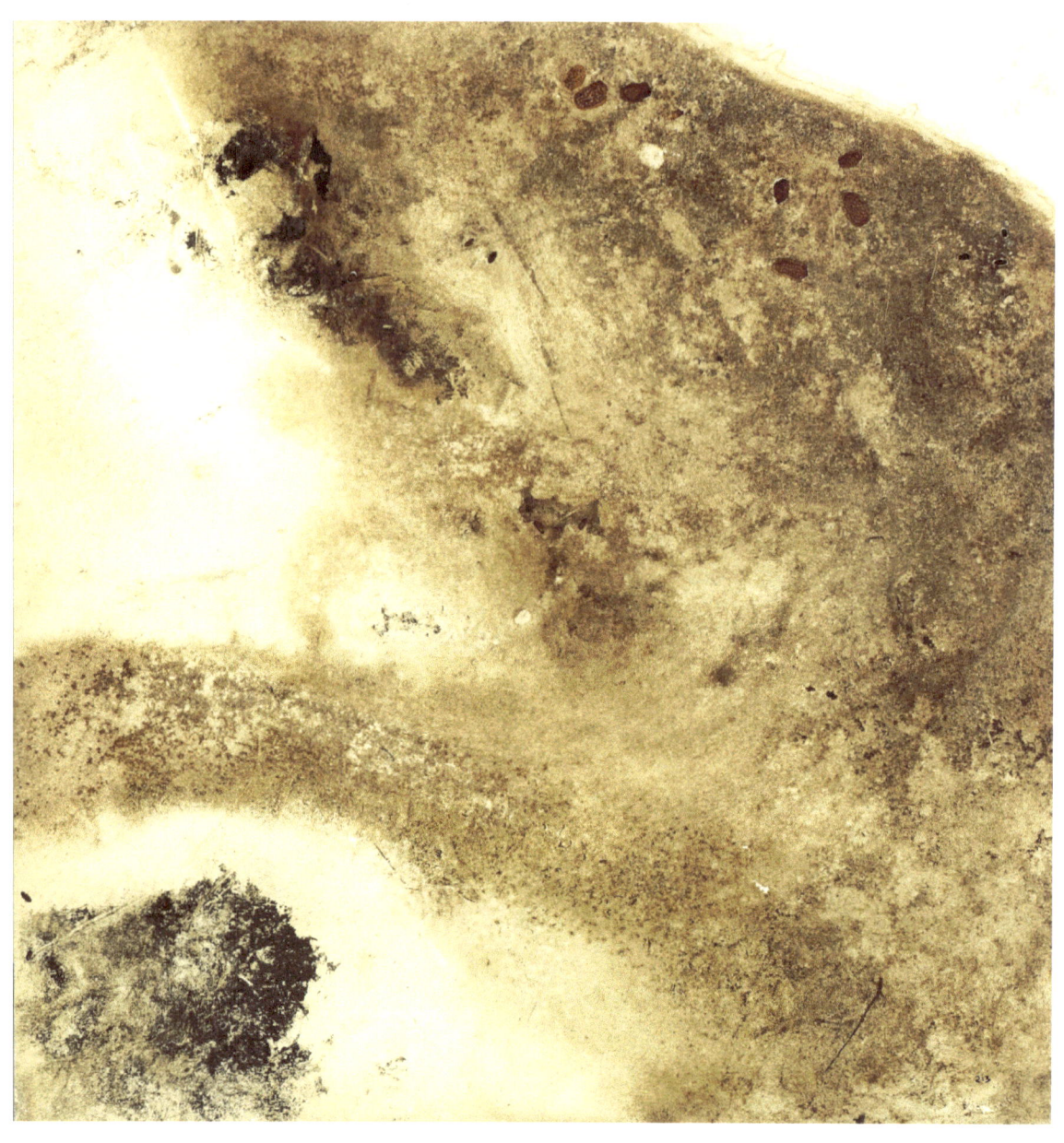

Nature No. 213

On the meadow near Höje River.
S.W. of Lund, Sweden. Oct 17- 28, 1978
558 mm x 498 mm. Watercolor paper.

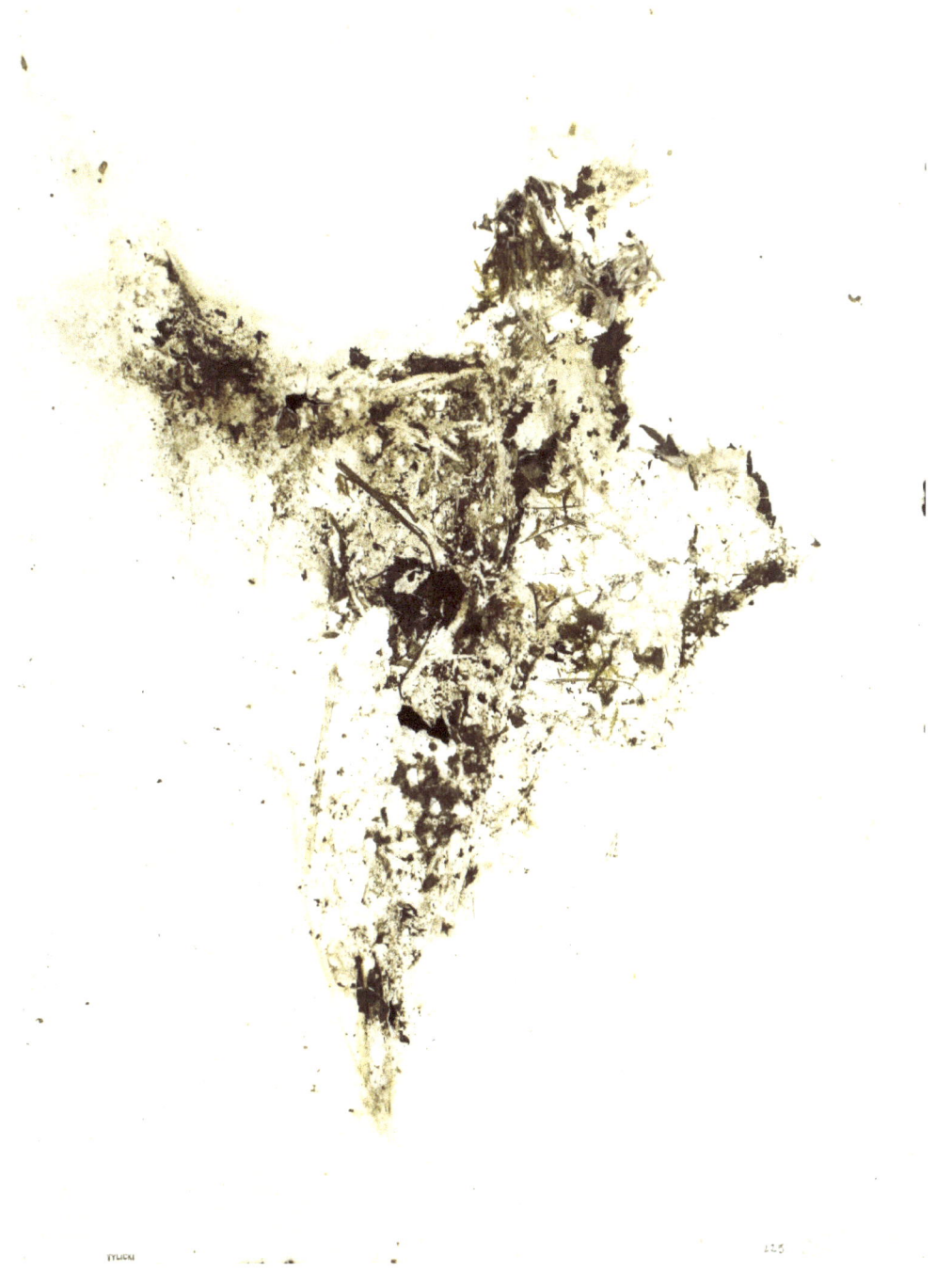

Nature No. 225

On a grass meadow.
S.W. of Lund, Sweden. Oct. 23 - Nov. 2, 1978
475 mm x 355 mm. Watercolor paper.

Nature No. 245

On a sandy meadow.
S.W. of Lund, Sweden. Oct. 29 - Nov. 12, 1978
475 mm x 355 mm. Watercolor paper.

Nature No. 343

On the forest meadow.
Sianowska Huta, near Kartuzy, Poland. May 09 – 29 1979
475 mm x 355 mm. Watercolor paper.

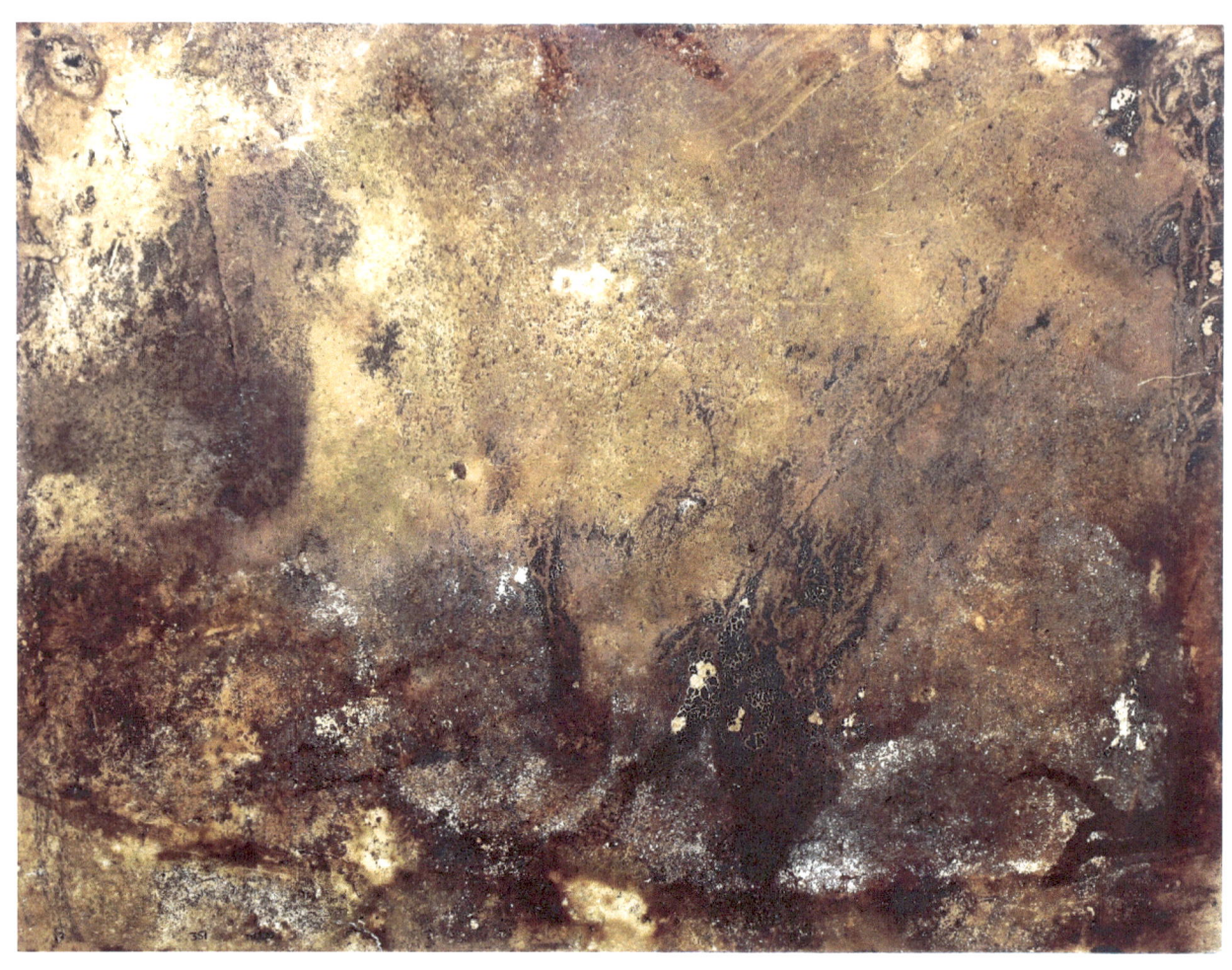

Nature No. 351

On the forest meadow.
Sianowska Huta, near Kartuzy, Poland. May 09 – 29 1979
475 mm x 355 mm. Watercolor paper.

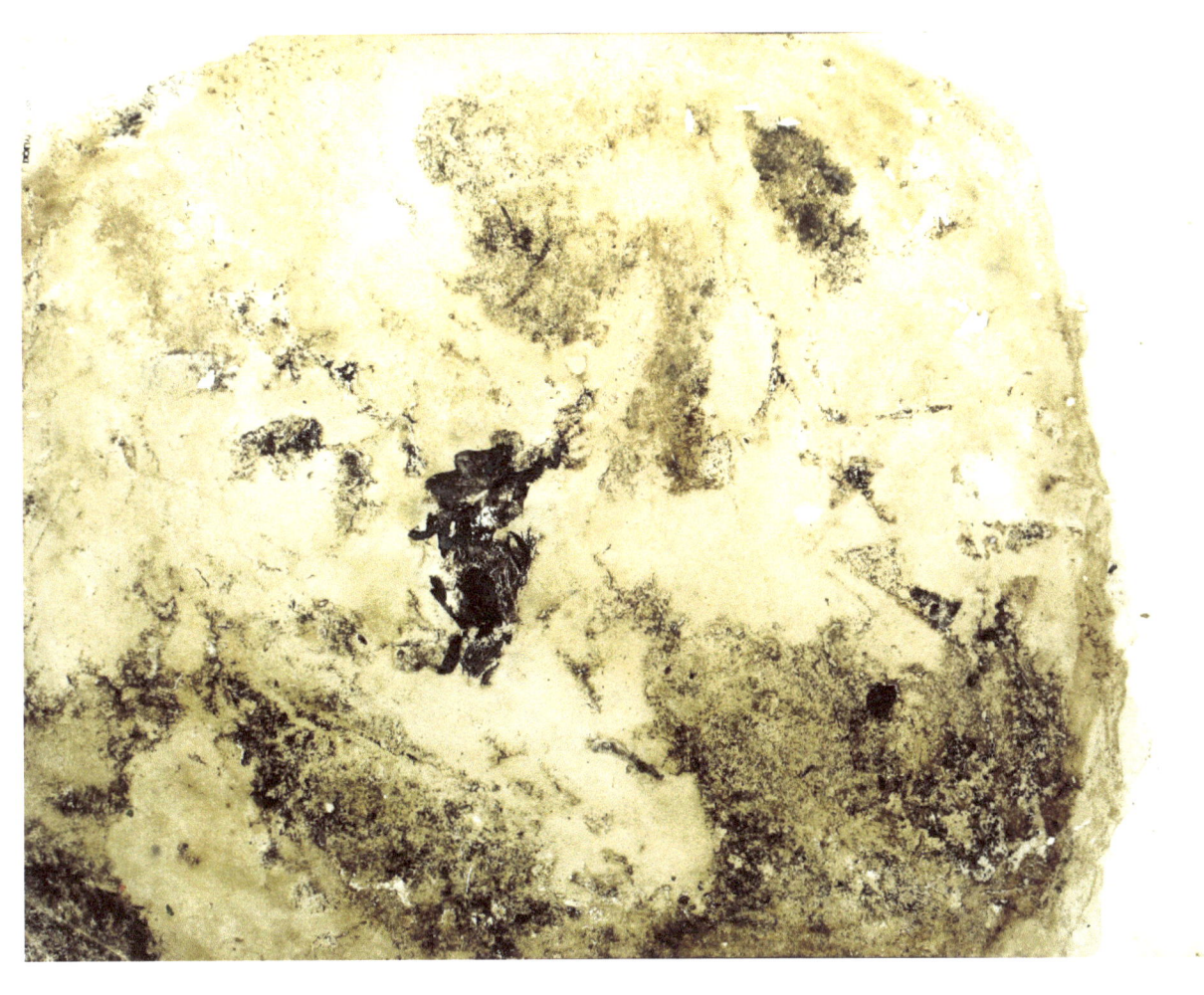

Nature No. 355

On forest meadow.
Sianowska Huta, near Kartuzy, Poland. May 12 – 26 1979
475 mm x 355 mm. Watercolor paper.

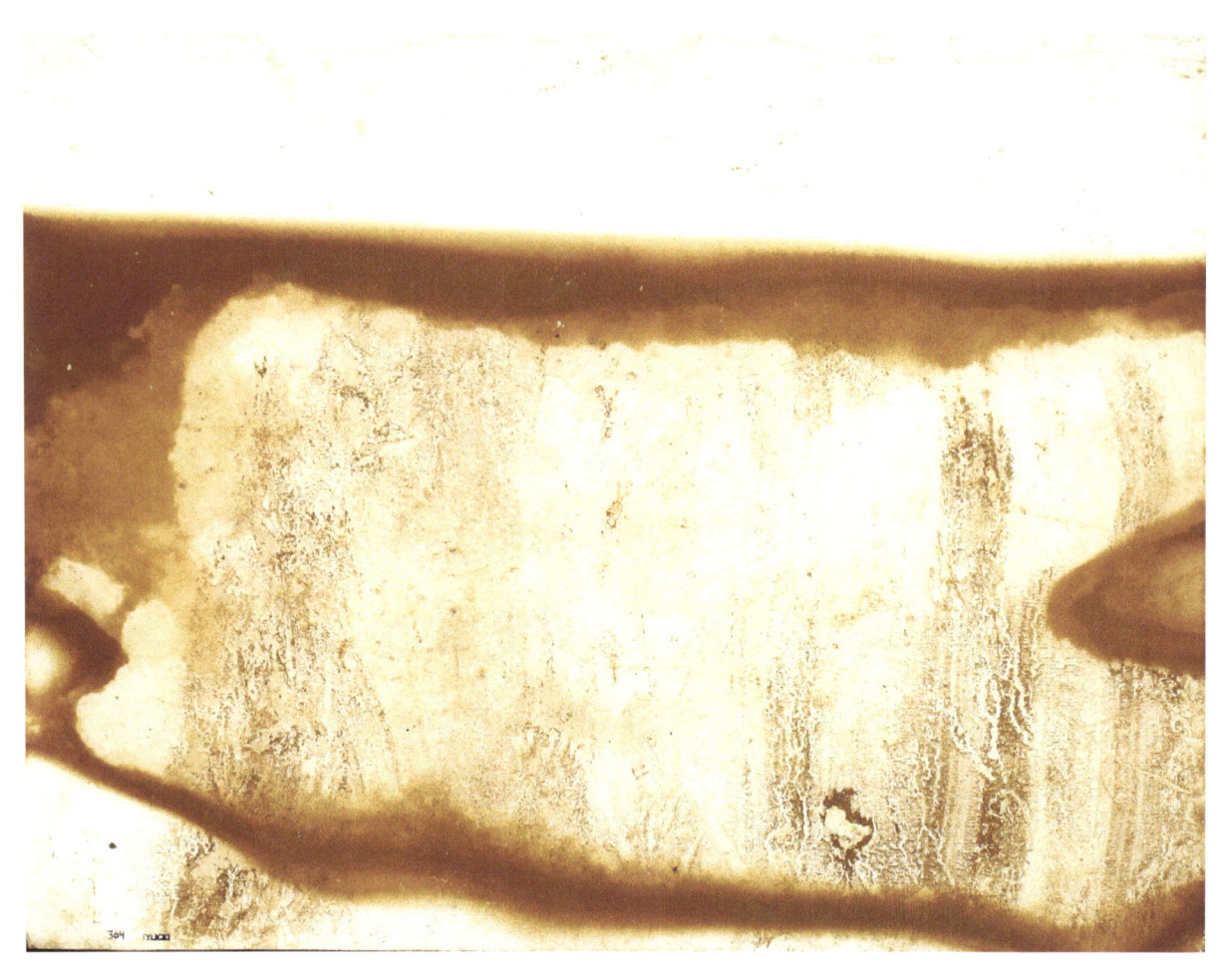

Nature No. 364

On volcanic meadow.
Ellidaar area, Iceland. June 29 - July 15, 1979
475 mm x 355 mm. Watercolor paper.

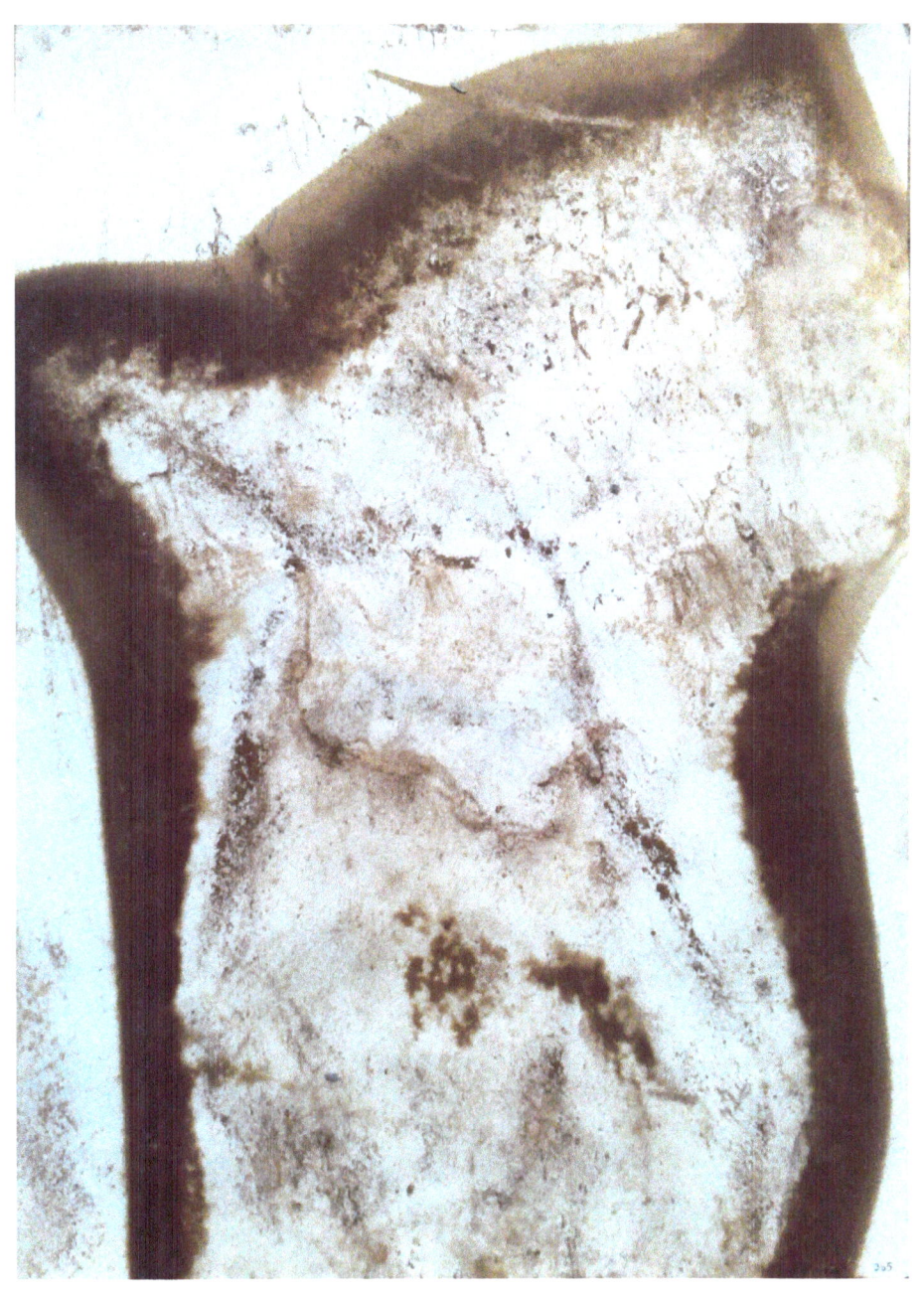

Nature No. 365

On volcanic ground.
Ellidaar area, Iceland. June 29 - July 15, 1979
475 mm x 355 mm. Watercolor paper.

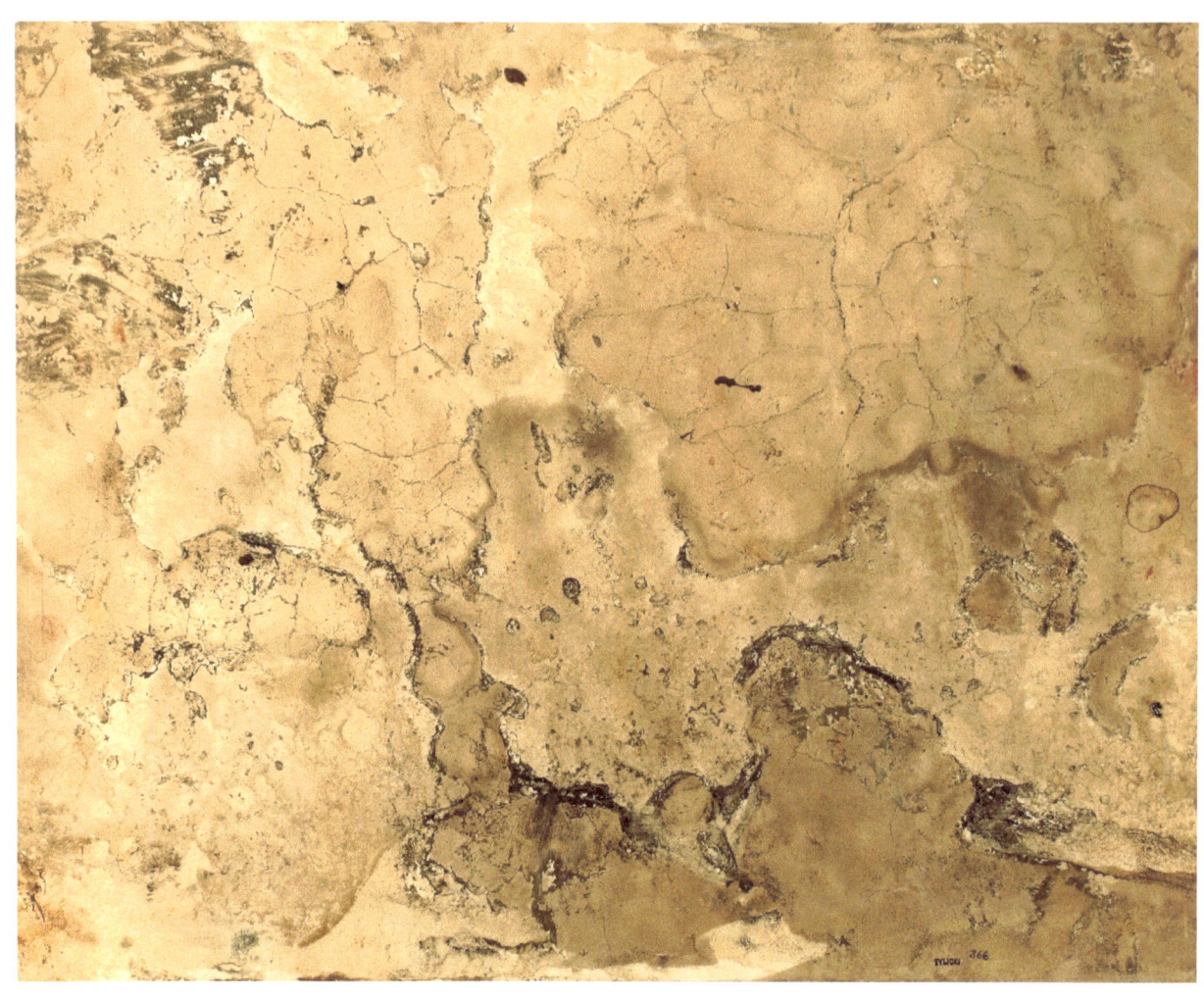

Nature No. 369

On volcanic ground.
Ellidaar area, Iceland. July 1 – 14, 1979
475 mm x 355 mm. Watercolor paper.

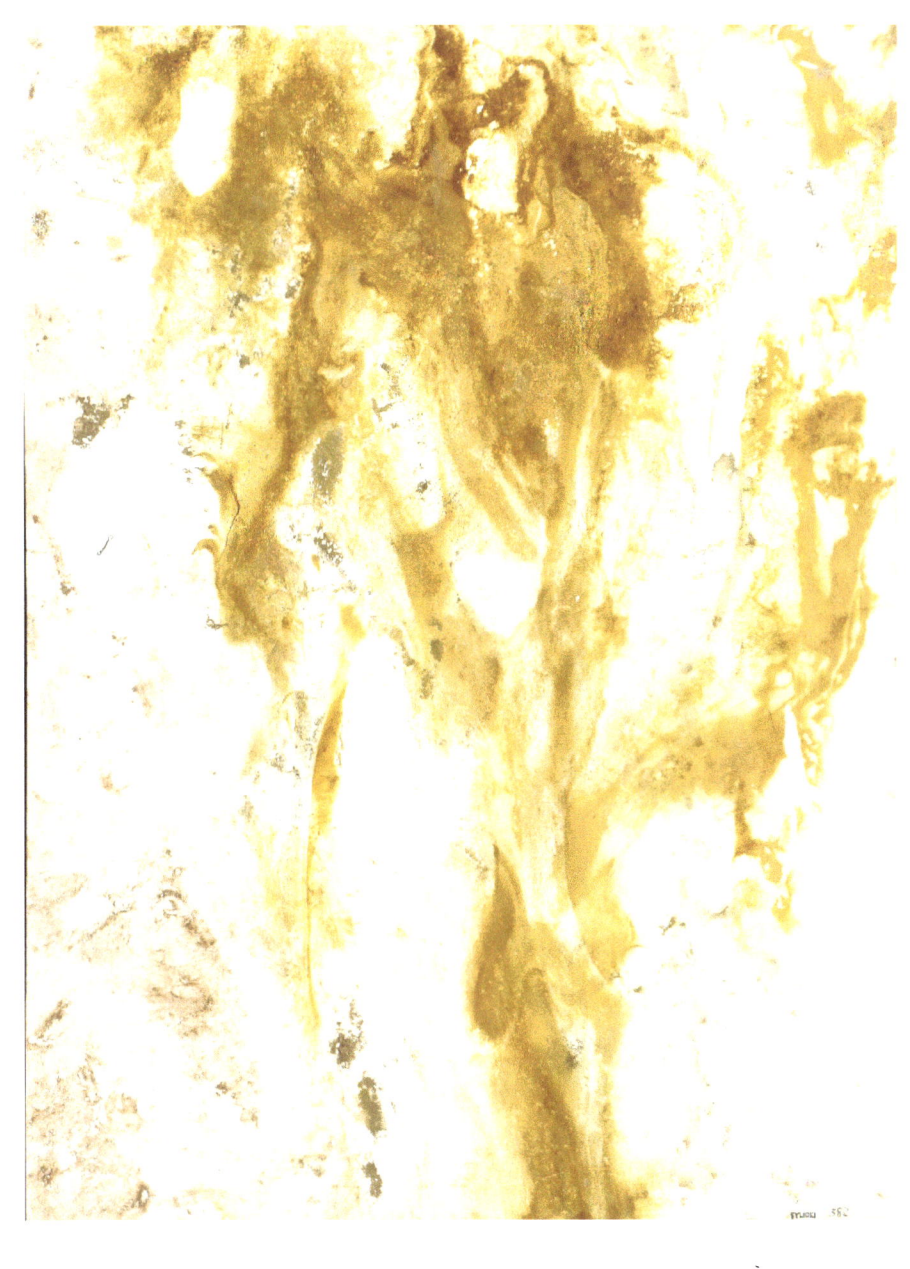

Nature No. 382

Near Krísuvík Hot springs.
Iceland. July 2 – 15, 1979
475 mm x 355 mm. Watercolor paper.

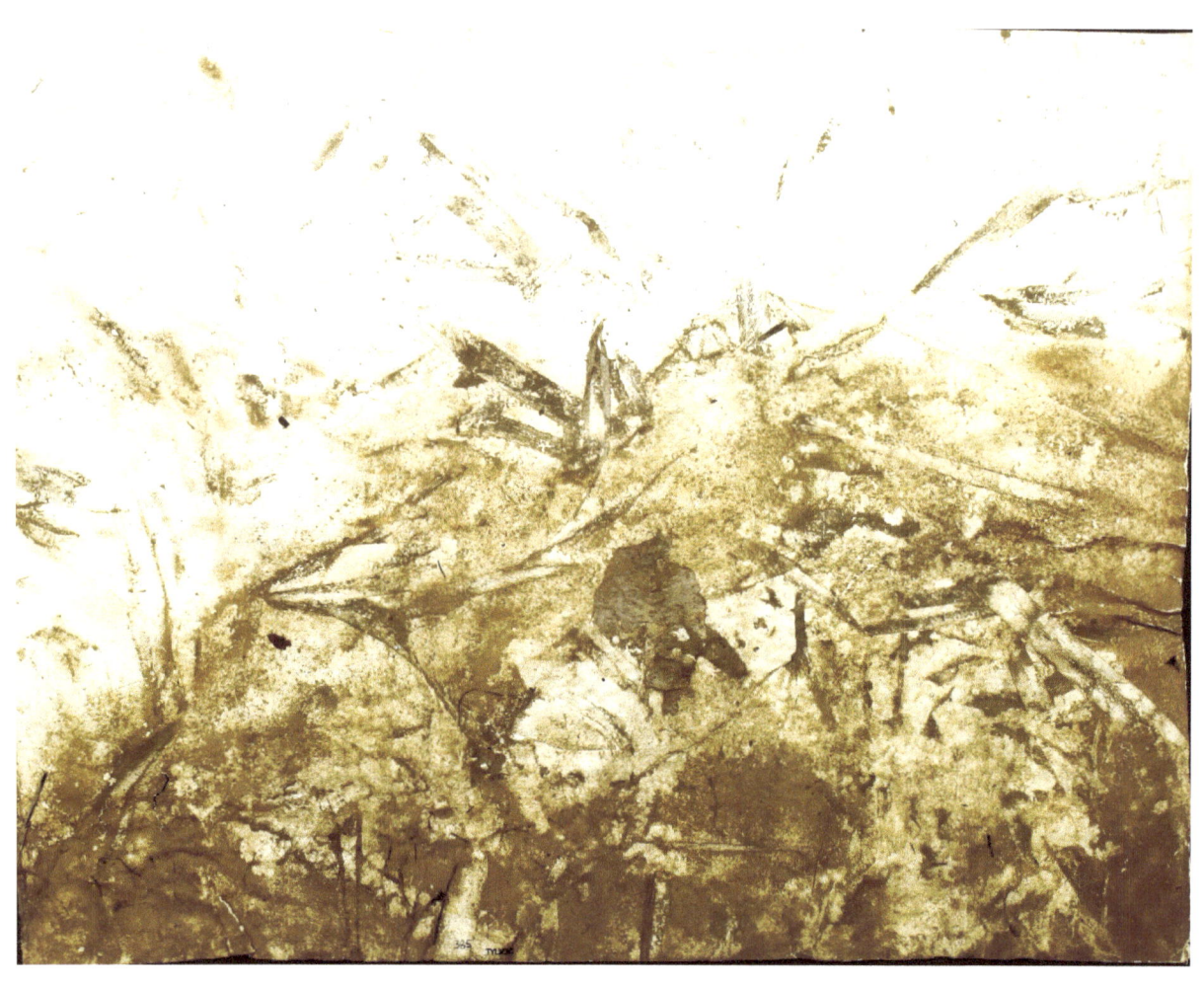

Nature No. 385

On the bank of Höje River.
S.W. of Lund, Sweden. Sep. 14 – 25, 1979
475 mm x 355 mm. Watercolor paper.

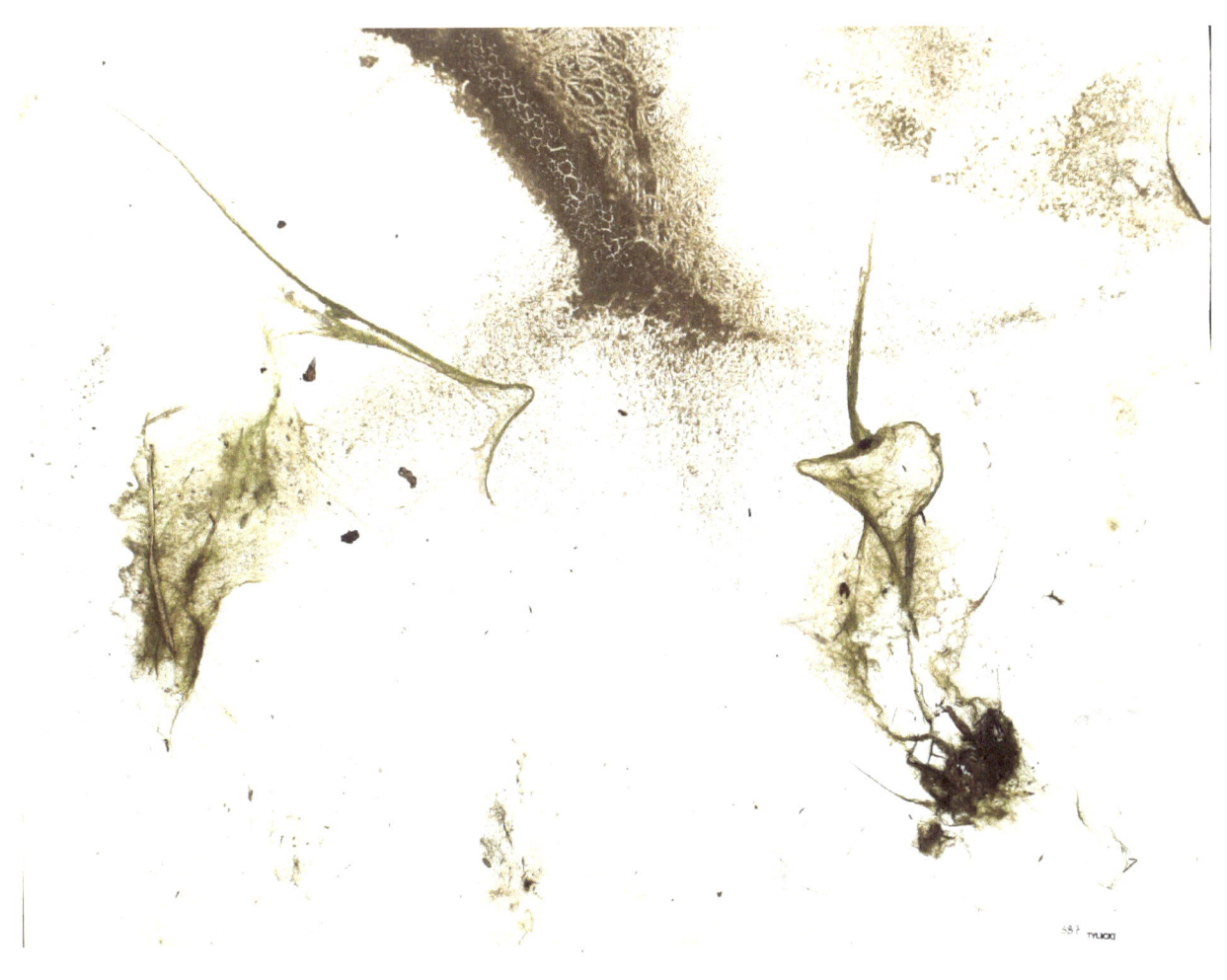

Nature No. 387

In the rushes of the Höje River.
S.W. of Lund. Sweden. Sep. 17 – 26, 1979
475 mm x 355 mm. Watercolor paper.

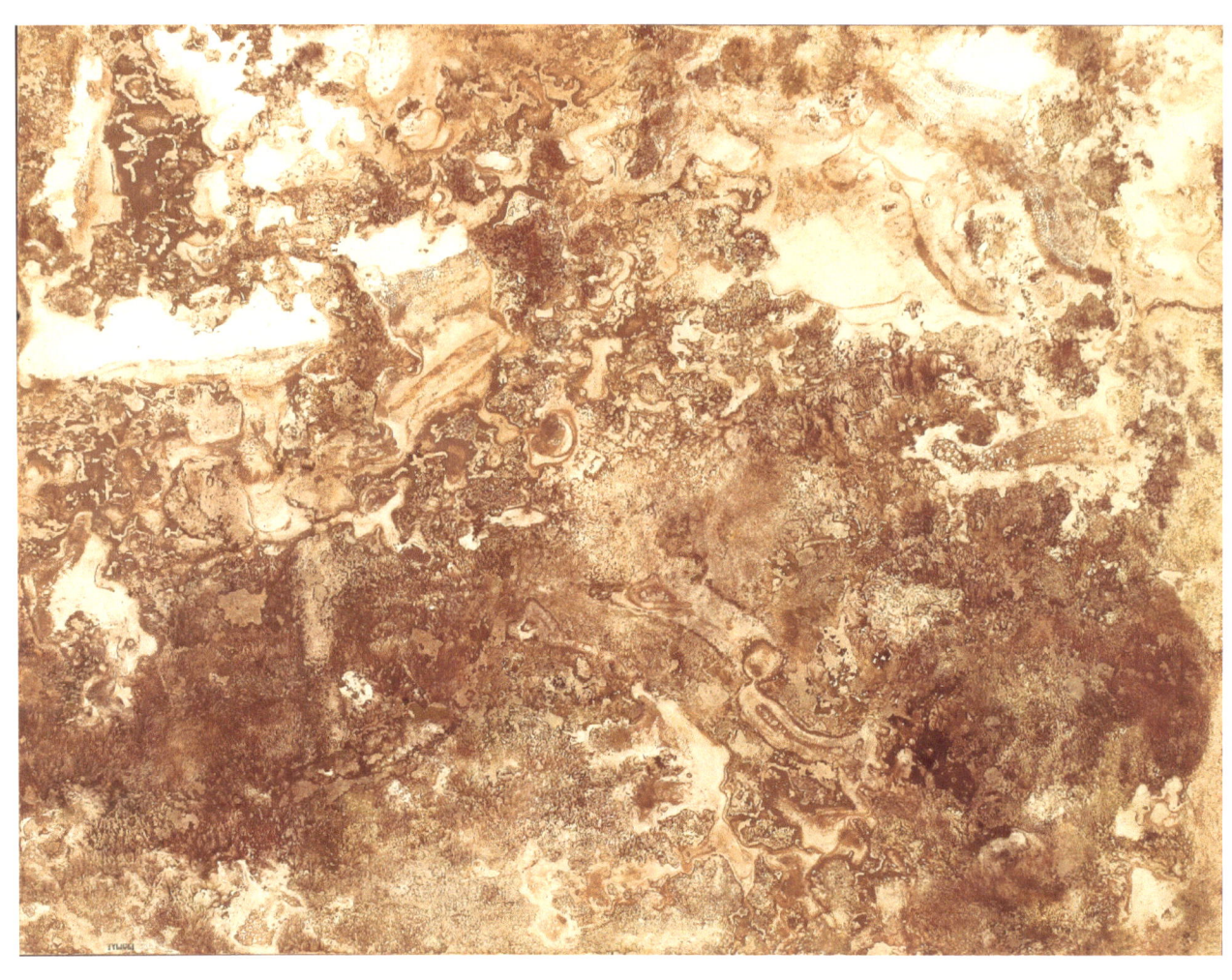

Nature No. 390

On volcanic ground.
Near Krisuvik, Iceland. July 2 – 15, 1980
475 mm x 355 mm. Watercolor paper.

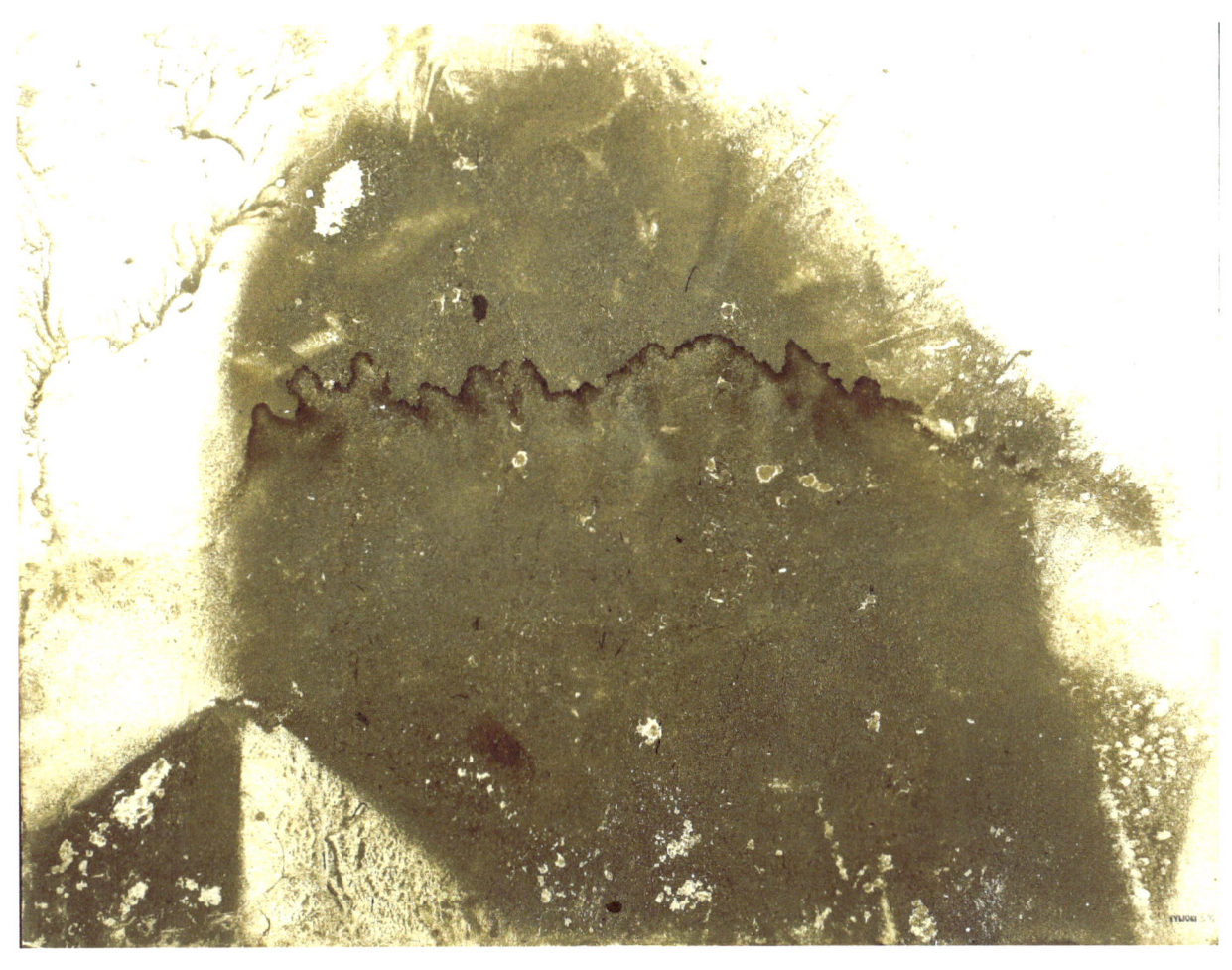

Nature No. 506

In the rushes of the Höje River.
S.W. of Lund, Sweden. May 02 - 06 1981
475 mm x 355 mm. Watercolor paper.

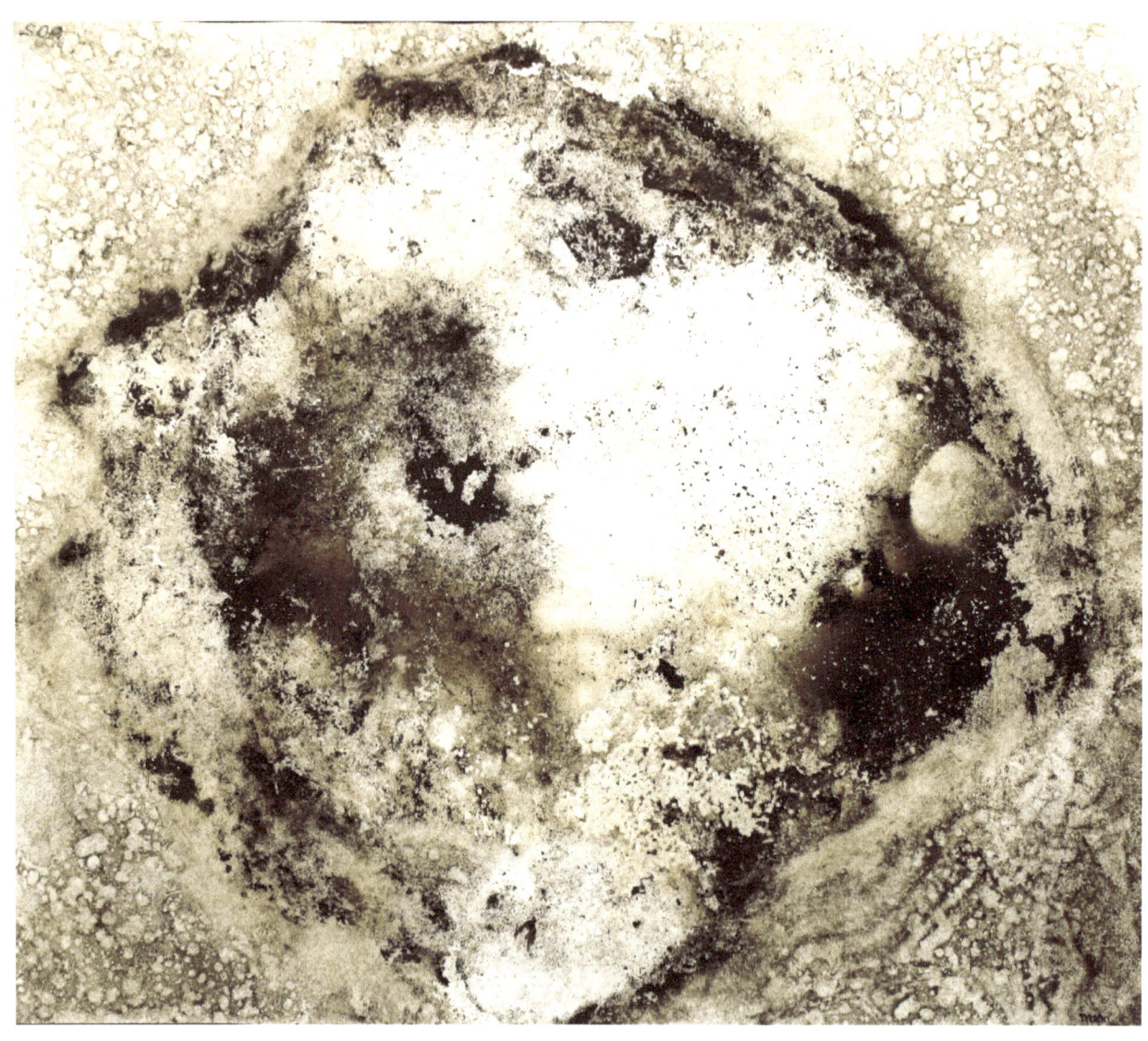

Nature No. 605

On the forest floor, among the stones and rain.
Frost Valley, Catskills, USA. Apr 29 - May 24, 1996.
419 mm x 381 mm. Watercolor paper.

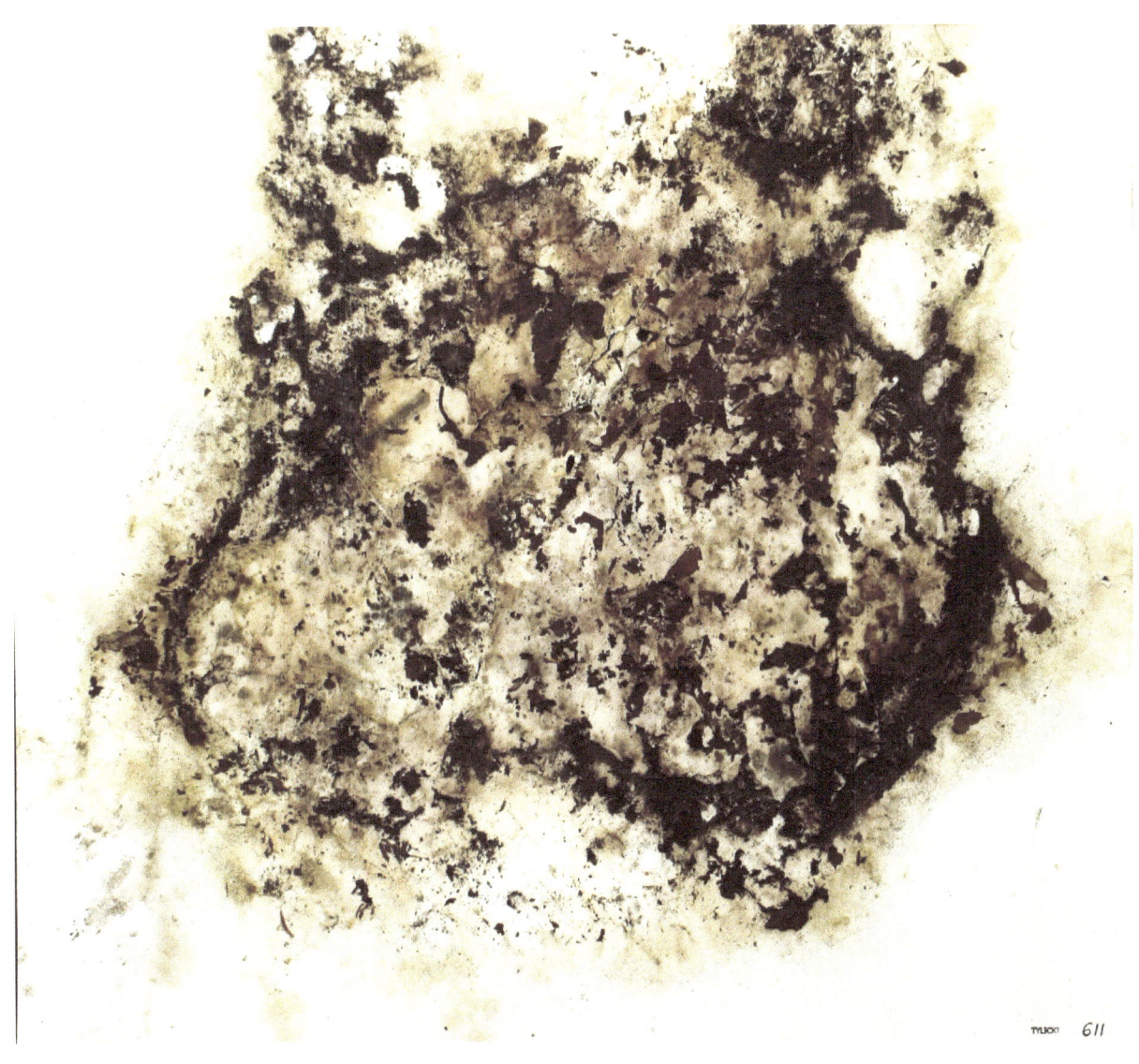

Nature No. 611

On the forest floor, among the stones and rain.
Frost Valley, Catskills, USA. May 12 - June 2, 1996.
419 mm x 381 mm. Watercolor paper.

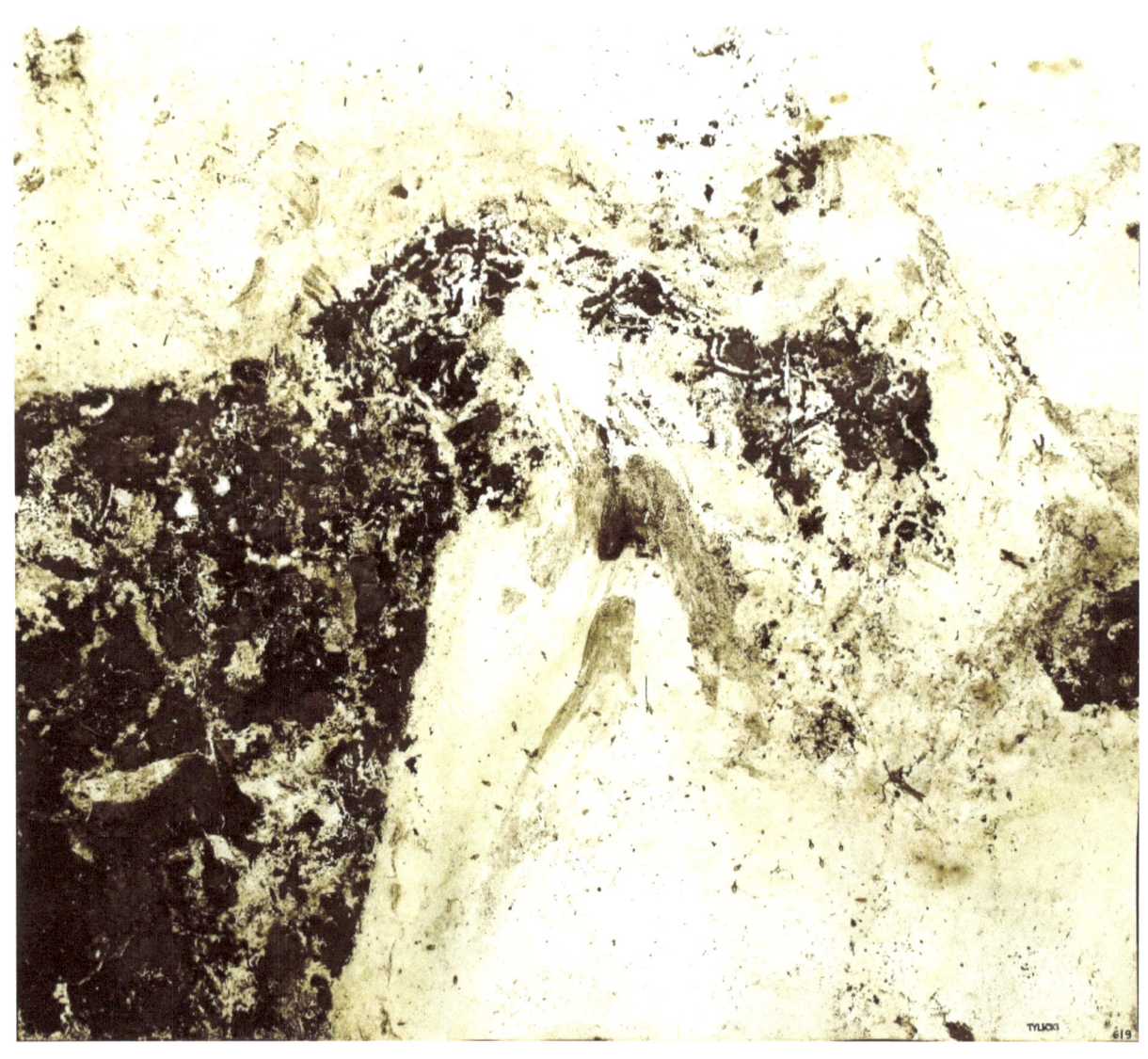

Nature No. 619

On the forest floor, among the stones and rain.
Frost Valley, Catskills, USA. May 21 - June 15, 1996.
419 mm x 381 mm. Watercolor paper.

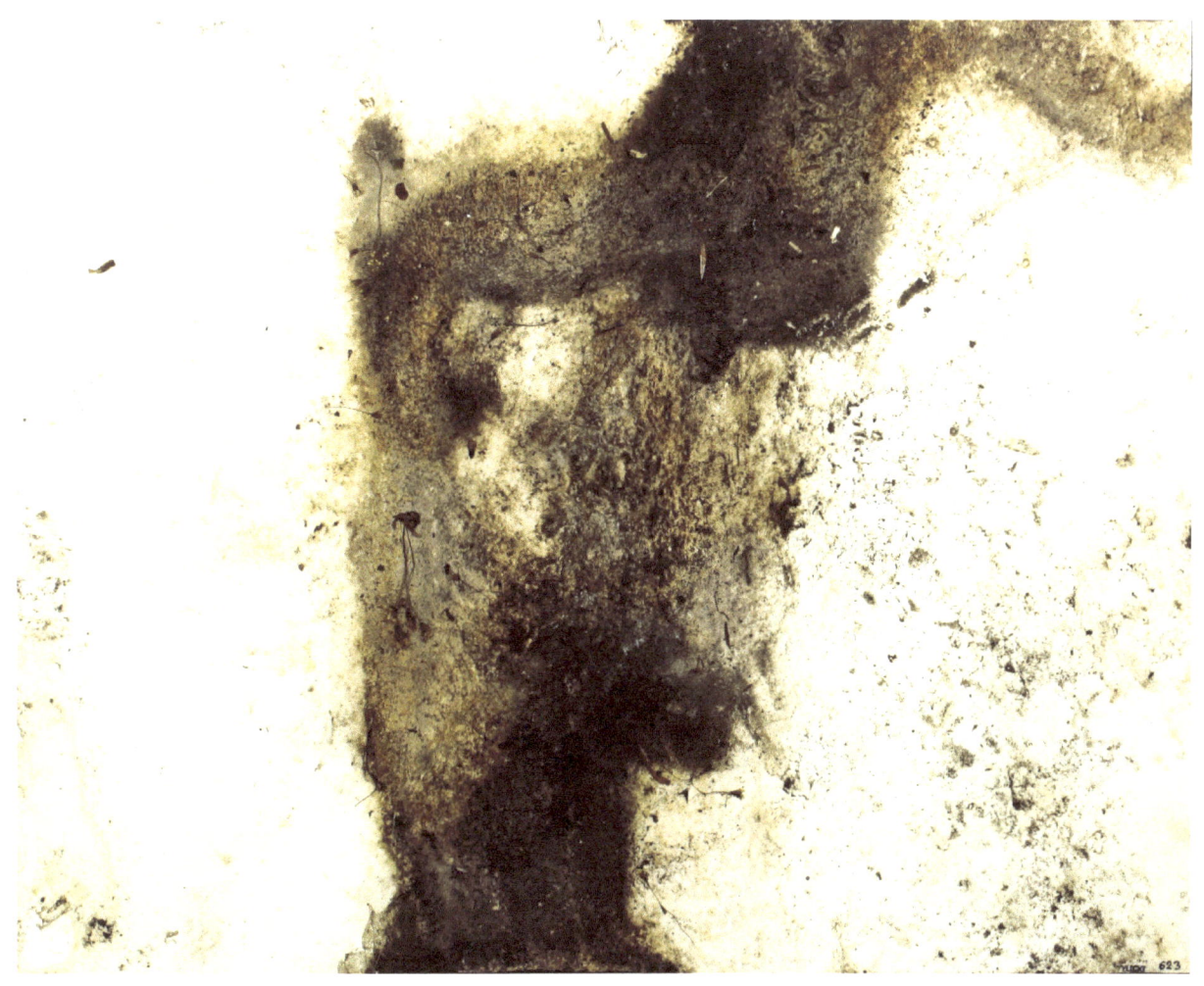

Nature No. 623

On the forest floor, among the stones and rain.
Frost Valley, Catskills, USA. May 21 - June 15, 1996.
419 mm x 381 mm. Watercolor paper.

Nature No. 901

On the ground of a forest. Near Sopot, Poland
Apr 12 – May 16 2012
143 cm x 214 cm. On canvas.

Nature No. 930

On the shore of a jungle river. Andaman Islands.
Dec 20 2013 – Jan 12 2014
320 x 320 mm. On canvas.

NOTES

[i] Jacek Tylicki, *Business as Art*.

[ii] Joseph Kosuth, *Art After Philosophy and After*, (*Collected Writings, 1966-1990)*. Ed. by G. Guercio, foreword by Jean-François Lyotard, MIT Press 1991, p. 20.

[iii] Tylicki, *Living in the Tree*.

[iv] The Guinness Book of Records 1984, (*Le livre Guinness des records 1984*), Paris 1983, p. 326.

[v] Arnold Hauser, *The Social History of Art*, vol. 2 (*Renaissance, Mannerism, Baroque*), Rutledge UK, London 1999, chapter 6.1.

[vi] Walter Benjamin, *The Work of Art in the Age of Mechanical Reproduction*, § IV; [in:] http://web.bentley.edu/empl/c/rcrooks/toolbox/common_knowledge/general _communication/benjamin.html

[vii] Immanuel Kant, *The Critique of Judgement*; translated with introduction and notes by J.H. Bernard, (revised edition Mac Millan and Co., London 1931), this edition: Read Books, London 2007, § 5, p. 55.

[viii] The Third Definition of Beauty, *ibidem*, § 17, p. 90.

[ix] *Ibidem*, § 49, p. 197

[x] see: The Ecological Problem as a Problem for Discourse Ethics, [in:] A. Ofsti (ed.), Ecology and Ethics, Melbu, Academie-Verlag 1992. K. -O. Apel, "Une éthique universaliste est-elle possible?", [in:] La philosophie en Europe, ed. by R. Kalibansky and D. Pears, Paris, Gallimard / UNESCO, 1993, p. 500. [in:] Paul Ricoeur, *Les métamorphoses de la raison herméneutique*, ed. by J. Greisch and R. Kearney, Paris, Ed. du Cerf 1991, pp. 117-122.

[xi] We must point here to an ambiguity, embedded in a translation of the German term "das Spiel", which in the English language forks off into two separate concepts of game and play; the first of these terms includes the combinatorial connotations of aleatory procedures ("games of chance"), while the second one implies spontaneity of the participants ("playful"). The German "das Spiel" carries both meanings.

[xii] Schiller, *op. citatum*, *Thirteenth Letter*, p. 69.

[xiii] *Ibidem*, *Fifteenth Letter*, p. 80.

[xiv] Johan Huizinga, *Homo Ludens* (a study of the play-element in culture) (1938), The Beacon Press, Boston 1955, p. 202.

[xv] Hans-Georg Gadamer, *Truth and Method*, A Continuum Book / The Seabury Press, New York 1975, chapter II, p. 91.

xvi Kosuth, [in:] *"Miedzy marzeniem sennym a ideologia: cztery luzne uwagi"* ("Between a reverie and ideology: four casual statements".), [in:] "Obieg" nr 61/62, May/June 1994, p. 4.

xvii Tylicki, *Chicken & Art*.

xviii Henri Bergson, *Laughter (An Essay on the Meaning of the Comic)*, transl. by C. Brereton, The MacMillan Company, New York 1912, p. 150.

xix Revolutions represent a change in the façade of the actual centers of power, which —in an unbroken state— ride the waves of revolutionary events.

xx Tylicki, *Make War in Art, not in Reality*.

xxi Wilhelm Dilthey, *The Essence of Philosophy*, (transl. by S.A. Emery and W.T. Emery (trans.), Chapel Hill: University of North Carolina Press, 1954, p.76.

xxii Dithey, *Gesammelte Schriften*, vol. V, Tübingen 1964, p. 168.

xxiii titles of the anthologies

xxiv Hubert Damisch, *Traité du trait*, Rúnion des Musées Nationaux, Paris 1995, p. 60. In French the word "stylo" (pen) is closely related to "stylet" (stiletto).

xxv Kant, *op. citatum*, § 28, p. 124.

xxvi "A fantastic wall ornament (Mondrian), an interesting design of an airport hall (Delaunay), or a fancy print of a summer dress (Buren)", writes Jean-Joseph Goux, an Associated Professor at Rice University in Houston; "Eclipse de l'Art?", "Esprit", October 1994, p. 106.

xxvii see for example: Charles Baudelaire, *Le Spleen de Paris*, Paris 1979, Poem XII, p. 86: "Ce que les hommes nomme amour est bien petit, bien restreint et bien faible, comparé à cette ineffable orgie, à cette sainte prostitution de l'âme qui se donne toute entiere, poésie et charité, à l'imprévu qui se montre à l'inconnu qui passe." Compare also: Walter Benjamin, *The Paris of the Second Empire in Baudelaire*.

xxviii [in:] *Sociologie et anthropologie*, (selected writings), Paris 1966, p. 173.

xxix There are similarities between gift and the principle of *potlatch*. Our "liberal realist" has not read an equally fascinating account of Bronislaw Malinowski's ethnographic journeys to The Trobriand Island. *Potlatch* represents a form of ceremonial exchanges between clans, in which an excessive extravagance verging on wastefulness reaches unimaginable proportions. The chiefs of tribes (or familial groups) give material objects, which are then publicly destroyed: the annual production of food, clothes, arms, and ornaments is burned, or sunk in the ocean. The recipients cannot refuse the gift — this would involve running the risk of losing their tribal position and offending the totemic ancestors, who grant them the power of leadership and valor; they are obliged to reciprocate the gift in the next *potlatch*. Potlatch can be regarded as a contradiction, or at least the reverse side, of the principle of profit, while its threefold system of responsibility: giving—receiving—reciprocating, successfully regulates certain forms of social behavior.

xxx *Vie et mort de l'image. Une histoire du regard à l'Occident*, Gallimard, Paris 1992, p. 63.

xxxi T. Atkinson, M. Baldwin, "On the Material-Character/Physical-Object Paradigm of Art" (1972); [in:] *Art-Language*. February, pp. 51-55.

xxxii *Art & Auction* Magazine

xxxiii Fred Forest, *Art sociologique*. Vidéo, Paris, 1977, pp. 91-94: "a sale at an auction of "one artistic square meter" [of land] under the hammer of the Master Auctioneer Binoche" — explains Forest —"was at the last minute interrupted and prevented by the intervention of the Court of Justice, for the reason of introducing an alleged conflict of competence between the public notaries and the official auctioneers. Only the notaries are, by law, authorized to sell land; but was the piece in question a parcel of land, or a work of art? An object of the transaction is then spontaneously exchanged for "a non-artistic square meter", a piece of *taivec* of the exactly same dimension, spread out at the entrance to the auction hall and previously trampled by the personnel. The final price at the auction will reach 130 times the price, at which it was purchased from the wholesale the morning of the auction."

xxxiv Boltansky most recently used similar tactics; in order to prevent speculation involving the books, published during the seventies, the author produced a series of authorized reprints in the quality of an original.

xxxv Johann Gottlieb Fichte, Contributions to the Correction of the Public's Judgment concerning the French Revolution (1793), (*Considérations sur la Révolution française*, French transl. by J. Barni, Payot, Paris 1974, p. 116).

xxxvi A perfect illustration of the present situation in the art market can be found in a book by Rainer Rochlitz, *Subvention et subversion*, Gallimard, Paris 1994.

xxxvii Ad Reinhardt, "Aesthetic responsibility" (1962) [in:] *Art as Art, (The Selected writings of Ad Reinhardt)*, ed. by B. Rose, University of California Press, 1991, p. 164.

xxxviii Wassyli Kandinsky, *Concerning the Spiritual In Art* (1910), transl. by M.T.H. Sadler, Dover Publications Inc., New York, pp. 53-55.

xxxix Friedrich Nietzsche, *On the Geneaology of Morals (a polemic)* (1887), transl. by B. Sammel, T.N. Foulis, Edinburgh & London, 1913; Third Essay: "What is the meaning of ascetic ideals?", pp. 121-123.

[xl] Tylicki, *Reconstruction Attempt of Korpfulsstadir Quarry*.

[xli] Tylicki, Chicken & Art; the portraits of chickens used in the New York installation by: Dima Sheinman, Dariusz Gubala, Denis @, and Jacek Tylicki. The ones in Sopot were by: Tylicki, J. Czerniawski, and J. Swieszewski.

[xlii] Gilles Deleuze and Félix Guattari, *Capitalism and Schizophrenia: Anti-Oedipus* (1972), A Richard Seaver Book/The Viking Press, New York, 1977.

[xliii] Hauser, *opus citatum*, p.320.

[xliv] Joris-Karl Huysmans, *Against Nature (Wrong Way)*, (1884); "After looking at artificial flowers which imitated nature, he longed to see natural flowers which would look like the artifice." Penguin Classics, London, revised edition (April 29 2003).

[xlv] Quoting after: P. Ryckmans, Les *"Propos sur la peinture" de Shitao*, Bruxelles, 1970, p. 64.

[xlvi] F. Dastur, De la phénoménologie trascendentale à la phénoménologie herméneutique, [in:] Paul Ricoeur, Les métamorphoses..., *op. citatum*, pp. 49-50

[xlvii] Gaston Bachelard, *The Poetics of Reverie (Childhood, Language, and the Cosmos),* translation by Grossman Publishers; Beacon Press, 1971, p.20

ABOUT THE AUTHOR

Prof. Leszek Brogowski (France)

Prof. Leszek Brogowski is the Chair of aesthetics and art studies at the Faculty of Arts, Lettres, Communication (Arts, Literature, Communication) University of Haute Bretagne in Rennes 2 in France. He also taught history of philosophy and aesthetics at the Faculty of Philosophy at the Sorbonne in Paris and the universities of Paris I, Paris X and Valenciennes. In 2000 he founded the University of Rennes 2 publishing house Éditions Incertain Sens, publishing a book of artists. He published dozens of articles in the press of artistic and philosophical in the country and abroad, including "Format", "Magazine of Art", "Les Cahiers du mnam", "Critique d'art", "Galerie l'Ollave" " poïétique Recherches "," Revue d'esthétique "," Critique. " In the years 1975-1986 had many solo exhibitions of photography, drawing and painting, including in Gdansk, Lublin, Bialystok, Paris, Lyon and Copenhagen. He is the author of books: The Art and the man (WSIP 1989), Art in transition (WSIP 1989), Dilthey. Conscience et histoire (Presses Universitaires de France, 1997), Afterimages and the ... Unism and "Theory of Vision" Strzeminski, word / picture of the territories in 2001.

Published by: 21UNIVERSE

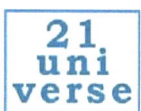

ISBN-13: 978-0985369231
ISBN-10: 098536923X

SPONSORED BY